At Peace with War

At Peace with War

A Chaplain's Meditations from Afghanistan

HAROLD RISTAU

WIPF & STOCK · Eugene, Oregon

AT PEACE WITH WAR
A Chaplain's Meditations from Afghanistan

Copyright © 2012 Harold Ristau. All rights reserved. Except for brief quotations in critical publications or reviews, no part of this book may be reproduced in any manner without prior written permission from the publisher. Write: Permissions, Wipf and Stock Publishers, 199 W. 8th Ave., Suite 3, Eugene, OR 97401.

Wipf & Stock
An Imprint of Wipf and Stock Publishers
199 W. 8th Ave., Suite 3
Eugene, OR 97401
www.wipfandstock.com

ISBN 13: 978-1-62032-370-0
Manufactured in the U.S.A.

Scripture quotations are from The Holy Bible, English Standard Version˚ (ESV˚), copyright © 2001 by Crossway, a publishing ministry of Good News Publishers. Used by permission. All rights reserved.

These journal excerpts are dedicated to all Canadian chaplains who have faithfully served overseas or supported the rear party back home.

"The nation which forgets its defenders will itself be forgotten"
(Calvin Coolidge)

LEST I FORGET

Undeserved though I be,
divine compassion shown to me.
Forgetting remains.
Mercy sustains.
Hell reveals.
Heaven conceals.
Undeserved though I stay,
neglecting, recalling, yesterday.

Preface

GEORGE ORWELL IS CREDITED with saying, "People sleep peaceably in their beds at night only because rough men stand ready to do violence on their behalf." It is easy to judge war while sitting on a couch and listening to reporters expressing their biased opinions through our television sets. Yet this quote reflects to me the necessity of warfare and the military. The legalized application of violence is a necessary evil. Nobody wants war. Nevertheless, sometimes, it is unavoidable. To say that Canadians ought not to fight in a war that has no immediate impact on our national self-interests is clearly selfish. Most of our military personnel realize this. The men, women and families of the Canadian, American, British and other coalition Forces sacrifice themselves daily to do the work of all the citizens of our nations in establishing better lives for those in need. Despite the pessimistic attitudes of many civilians in regards to our foreign affairs, there have been changes for the better. After being deployed twice to Afghanistan, I have witnessed them with my own eyes. Still, these changes come at a cost.

The reflections recorded in this book are derived from the journal that I kept after spending approximately 300 days in theater, working with both the Army and Air Force. As a chaplain I spent several months working in the hospital on the main base on KAF, and also worked with medics on the front line. I have been deployed outside the wire to all sorts of bases: from medium size FOBs consisting of anywhere between one to three hundred troops, to tiny Strong Points or House Platoons in which approximately a dozen Canadians abide. As a Christian chaplain, I cannot but help to filter the world through the eyes of my faith, nor would I want to see it in any other way. Accordingly, these writings do not only offer insights into our Armed Forces' experience in Afghanistan, they also manifest the devotional reflections of a Lutheran pastor. I have discovered spiritual treasures tucked away in the lives and experiences of the common soldier. These soldiers are a priesthood, practising a vocation as holy as any other. Although some sadly regard them as sub-human killers, I believe that they bring to us insights into a divine language that some lack the courage to hear.

Publishing a journal while our troops are still deployed is a delicate matter for an officer of the Canadian Forces, due to the possibility of breaching security measures that could put at risk the lives of our soldiers. For this reason, I have included only the entries which could not, in any way, jeopardize our ongoing mission in Afghanistan. Furthermore, for the most part, I have not used the real dates or places in order to protect the identity of those that have served, and shared, with me.

Glossary

AO: Area of Operation. Each NATO Force is designated a certain region of the country for which it is responsible.

DFAC: Large cafeterias on KAF.

KAF: Kandahar Air Field. One of the main NATO bases in Afghanistan from which most operations are led.

CoC: Chain of Command. Every member and unit of the military is responsible to a hierarchical arrangement of supervisors and officers.

FOB: Forward Operation Bases. Bases within an area of operation that consist of anywhere from a couple to a few hundred personnel.

IED: Improvised Explosive Device. Massive mines constructed of yellow household jugs of cheap and easily accessible yet dangerous chemicals. The mines are hidden beneath roads, in trees, under bridges or in walls of compounds, and are designed to explode when an individual or vehicle triggers the pressure plate.

CF: Canadian Forces.

CO: Commanding Officer of a military unit.

Padre: A synonym for chaplain. It is Spanish for "Father."

SOP: Standard Operating Procedures are military rules.

ROE: Rules of Engagement determine the limits and freedoms of the use of violence. They may change many times during the course of a mission based on developments in the war.

OTW: Outside The Wire. Large bases are surrounded by barbed wire or sand walls. Risk and danger increase significantly on the other side of those barriers.

Ramp Ceremonies: A funeral-like parade commemorating the deceased members of the Armed Forces prior to their shipment home. Before leaving the KAF, public prayers are offered, bagpipes are played and a eulogy is read while the body is carried up the ramp of the aeroplane, offering soldiers a last chance to say goodbye. Normally representatives of all allies are present. During battle seasons, these ceremonies may occur several times in a day.

RPG: Insurgent rockets usually bought from China or the former Soviet Union.

Pashtun: An ethnic group located in South-Western Afghanistan. *Pashtuns* pay no allegiance to either Afghanistan or Pakistan, and have been labelled "the devils of the desert" for their ability to conquer foreign armies with minimal technology. Most of the insurgents, such as the Taliban, belong to this cluster of tribal groups.

SAF: Small Arms Fire.

Theater: Another way of saying "in the battlefield."

Jirga: Local community meetings in which the decisions made by the majority are binding on the rest.

KIA: Killed in action.

LAV: A military vehicle designed for transporting troops.

War Diary

AUGUST 3

JUST A FEW FEET outside the building where I sleep lie the graves of two small children. Their bodies are covered with a blanket, but their bones have begun to pierce through the material after having been exposed to the elements over the last six years. When the Canadian soldiers first arrived here, they found the children hanging in this old abandoned school in which we now sleep. With them were dozens of deteriorating corpses of other Afghan children, slaughtered by the Taliban. Their crime? They attended school. Now they are buried on the other side of the compound . . . in a mass grave.

How blessed we are in our own country, where we are free to vote, read, and think. The Taliban are their own worst enemy, for these sorts of stories are not easily forgotten in a country as old as Afghanistan. Feuds are remembered for generations. Insults are punished with execution. Most of the Afghans despise the violent displays of tyrannical tribes. At the same time, a handful of gangsters in a village with only a couple of weapons will demand submission from these otherwise peaceful people. Many will show their support to whomever poses the greatest threat to the interests and honor of the clan. Decisions at the *jirgas* are binding to all.

Yet, behind closed doors, people continue to learn and judge for themselves. Children beg for pens and paper, not candy. The heads of the homes pray for the day when schools and hospitals will be safe. When I was an inner-city pastor in Montreal, Québec, prior to joining the military, I was constantly impressed by the determination to learn exhibited by refugees and immigrants from the Middle East. Women would often take the *Holy Injil* (New Testaments) from our literature table, and hide them under their *burkas*. They are eager to learn that which is forbidden them. History has repeatedly taught that attempts at controlling the minds of a people are futile. The resistance will overtake them . . . eventually. It only takes a little education. No wonder that a school represents the greatest of all threats.

Lord God, from whom all blessings flow, I praise You for the wisdom that we receive from wise and godly teachers. May You bless the development of schools and educators in Afghanistan to enlighten minds and enrich the lives of those who abide in dark places. In Jesus' name, Amen.

AUGUST 10

TODAY A FLIGHT ENGINEER was crushed by the ramp of a Chinook helicopter. Sometimes accidents just happen, and there is nobody to blame. His anti-fragment vest saved his life. These are plates that we wear on our back and front to absorb bullets and shrapnel from an explosion. Recently the CF has included armor for the throat, neck and shoulders. Heavy: Yes. Uncomfortable: Certainly. Necessary: Absolutely! Every time I arm myself, I am reminded of the full armor of God that we have received in Holy Baptism. Although I too am guilty, it still annoys me when Christians forget about this armor, or get lazy in putting it on. It is a question of spiritual life or death. I am equally bothered when Christians think that the armor isn't entirely and completely theirs from the day of their salvation, and that they accumulate more or better armor, through time, based upon rewards from the Holy Spirit. In the army, when we are issued our "kit," we get it all at once. There is some instruction on its usage, and certainly we are responsible for its upkeep (which is the same for our spiritual equipment through catechetical instruction and the Christian walk). But at the end of the day, there is nothing that *we* can say we have done well. The equipment is efficacious in itself. As St. Paul says, we have no reason to boast in the matter of spiritual warfare, since it is the equipment that has kept us safe and saved (I Corinthians 1:29).

Incidentally, there will still be wounds. That flight engineer broke some ribs. And we need to remember that there are still consequences of our spiritual battles with the world, our own flesh and the devil. We may break some spiritual ribs as well along the way. Jacob wrestled with

God. He went home blessed, but with a limp. Christians are persecuted for their faith. All of us have crosses to carry and thorns that we bear in the flesh. Christian suffering is a constant reminder that we are not yet in heaven, that we must continually rely on the Lord for all things. Without these involuntarily episodes of "fasting," we can quickly lose our appetite for heavenly things. Our Host, after all, has gone to great lengths to prepare us that meal. Moreover, He is a Lord who has Himself undergone all that we have undergone. No one has hungered and thirsted as He has. Christ has Himself suffered to heal us in our own sufferings. He knows the narrow way, for He has walked it before.

That flight engineer went home a changed man: praising those who designed and provided him with that safety equipment, and never forgetting his vulnerability without it. As one general once said, "it is well that war is so terrible, else we should grow too fond of it." This applies to the Christian battle as well. Our wounds, pains and sufferings keep us humble, and well focused on eternity. Our glimpses of heaven must never distract us from our mission on earth. For ours is an eternity that has been gained and shaped by nothing less than the sufferings of Christ.

Lord Jesus our Savior, thank You for the gracious protection that You provide us every day. Help us, with the help of the Holy Spirit, to treasure the spiritual armor that You have purchased and won for us through Your death and resurrection. Amen.

AUGUST 14

THIS MORNING AT 0600, about one hundred and fifty of us participated in the Terry Fox run. Most of our troops are out in the field, OTW, and don't have the luxury of these kinds of morale boosters. But for us on KAF, it delivers a welcome break in the week, and offers an opportunity to raise money for cancer research at the same time. Terry Fox is a Canadian hero. Thirty years ago, he attempted to run across the country with one artificial leg. He covered about 40 km a day. The interesting thing about him, and the part I love, is that he never finished the race. He died out West. Curiously, despite his failure, he remains a hero. History is filled with stories of glorious victories, especially in the athletic world. However, how many countries celebrate someone who, put bluntly, lost the race and never achieved his or her goal? It is more accurate to life though, isn't it? I once participated in a university debate with a Muslim academic. He cried out how he hated the fact that all the Biblical heroes were simultaneously failures in their ministries. What kind of a model did they set for us? Not a model of our capabilities, but rather of that which we are incapable of doing. "And isn't that wonderful!" I responded. Christ also looked liked a loser, His victory hidden from those who chose not to believe. No wonder the Muslims deny His crucifixion, claiming that He escaped death and lived a long healthy life for ninety years thereafter.

By the way, Terry Fox died *because* of the race. In short, had he never begun, he would have lived a longer life. He sacrificed himself for an important cause. And I guess, that is what we are celebrating with him. Not a victory, but a sacrifice. Of course, it is an ending that many Canadians choose to ignore, but for us Christians, it is typological of our Savior, and our soldiers. Although life is improving in this country of Afghanistan, the war will likely never end. It has been fought for thousands of years. War reminds us of our temporal existence, and our need for forgiveness. In Afghanistan, our mission is not simply about winning. And our soldiers go home heroes, especially the wounded ones, even though they never reached the finish line.

Victorious Savior, help us to trust Your Word that we are winners over sin, death and the devil, even when our experiences and the voices of our enemies attempt to convince us otherwise. Amen.

AUGUST 23

IT WAS AN EXCEPTIONALLY long ramp ceremony this afternoon. Nine Americans are dead. What made it particularly unsettling was that this time, for the first time in Afghanistan, a Chaplain and his assistant were among the casualties. It was bound to happen eventually—statistical probability. But when it happens to a colleague, it hits home hard. Could it have been me? I suppose. But, again, I remember Jesus saying something about picking up a cross and following him, and being willing to lay our lives down for our callings. Most of the disciples had similar fates. The ancient practice of having clergy lay on the ground in cruciform during the liturgy of ordination is an appropriate symbol of pastoral ministry. So why, then, are we so surprised when a clergyman is murdered in inner city ministry, or a missionary imprisoned in a communist country, or a chaplain killed in the line of duty? We have forgotten our first love, our *raison d'être*, that we are called to die; to die to self daily and, when it pleases our heavenly Father, to lay down our life for the Church. It sure is hard when you have a wife and four kids. And so my obligations, my duty and calling to my family and my ministry, conflict. I would prefer to "bury my father" before following Jesus. Can't I have it both ways Lord? You want me right away? But why? At the end of the day, the answer isn't ours to give, and our families need to be constantly reminded that they live in the shadow of the cross . . . of their dad.

> *Loving Shepherd, we chaplains are called to tend Your flock in the war zone, even though this vocation requires us to leave our families at home alone. Surround our loved ones with Your caring presence and protection, feeding them the Gospel through faithful pastors in supportive congregations and chapels. In Your holy name, Amen.*

AUGUST 25

TODAY I FEEL DISCOURAGED, lost, and awkward. It is rather strange trying to fit in when carrying the cross on our epaulets (i.e. ID "flaps"), especially amongst all these strangers. It wasn't that long ago that we arrived, so I guess this is all normal. While at the same time, the chaplain has it harder, due to the fact that one of our jobs is to simply "fit in." This can be difficult when all conversations eventually lead to sex and dirty jokes, at least amongst our younger, less mature military members. Still, my job is spending time with the troops and getting to know them, so that they trust me enough to come to me with their problems when the inevitable crisis occurs. Otherwise, my position is redundant while the member seeks advice and consolation with others in their CoC; friends with whom they feel more at ease to share their concerns; friends who may not be the most qualified to offer sound advice. Padres are aware of the dangers of befriending those whom they are called to father. For this reason, Christian ministry is often lonely. But even though healthy barriers need to be preserved, we are social with those whom we serve.

And when people are not struggling with personal issues, such as at the beginning of a tour when morale is relatively high, there is not that much for me to do, *except* to be social. On those days, I spend my time walking the line, and participating in conversations about ethics, politics, and God. But more often than not, I share in a lot of small talk. This is more important than you might think. I deliberately listen for news of potential issues that I may need to pursue in the future. If a member is already having trouble with his fiancée after only two weeks in theater, I can almost count on his visit into my office in the weeks to follow. But normally, on the slow days, I just make my face visible, make myself accessible, so that others see me and remember me. And when the wife threatens to terminate the marriage, the son overdoses on drugs, or the mother is checked into the hospital, these same people will come and find me *first*. In short, a lot of patience is required while waiting for emergencies to strike.

Unlike other trades, ours is not clearly defined. Sometimes we are described as "morale boosters." This could be considered the lowest common denominator unifying chaplains of various religions and confessions. But even this is over-emphasized. If you are having a bad day, the chaplain could be the prettiest cheerleader or funniest mascot, yet his or her smile or word of encouragement will have little lasting effect. Some commanders believe that the chaplain is the "pulse of the troops." This too is highly unrealistic, since the section leaders, or Sergeant Major, work much closer to their troops every day, and are better able to accurately determine whether or not group morale is high or low. What is my role? God knows. After all, He's the one who created the position, and called servants to fill it.

When I am not busy with cases, I may find myself helping other trades: carrying a radio or med kit on a convoy, loading and unloading supplies, cleaning, helping cook or serving in the kitchen, etc. Again, my motive is not purely to be helpful, but to be visible. Nevertheless, even when I am busy with cases, I am potentially replaceable by a social worker, with the exception that I usually offer a short prayer at the end of the session. The members are usually very happy, but that is incidental. Unfortunately, due to the decline of interest in Christianity, the religious aspect is not usually essential to my trade, which brings me back to my original point of feeling out of place and lost. At least sometimes. But perhaps, as pastors, it is appropriate that we feel ourselves awkward in our calling. A seminary professor once told our classes, "the moment that you are comfortable in the pulpit, is the moment that you shouldn't be there." Maybe the same applies for chaplains. The uncomfortable strangeness is reflective of an innate sensitivity we have to our high calling; that we are not *supposed* to be there; that no one is! No sinner, that is. It is, after all, the office *of Christ*. And yet, we have been chosen by God and called by His church. Naturally, we are to fear and revere the God of whom we are ambassadors. It is an office that should not be entered into or practised lightly or with great human ease. Perhaps, intuitively, Christian ministers like myself know and sense this, despite all of our attempts and self-convincing to normalize the job. Because it is established by God Almighty, it will never be robbed of its divine uniqueness. In short, we will never, totally, "fit in."

So, there I am, not knowing what I am supposed to be doing at most given times, or how to respond to any particular crisis. What words should I use to console that desperate wounded soldier? It is not necessarily negative. The Bible says that God's power is made perfect in our weakness (II Corinthians 12:9). Am I not a walking, talking, breathing, and living example of that promise? And so, "He must increase, but I must decrease" (John 3:30), to use the words of John the Baptizer. I refuse to throw around too strongly the phrase attributed to Francis of Assisi: "preach the Gospel and when necessary use words," since it can be an easy cop out when we do not want to say something meaningful even when we ought to say it. We will never become more popular by proclaiming the hope that is within us. Yet the point is well taken that sometimes, it's not *what you say*, but *who you are* that counts. Occasionally, it is appropriate not to say anything. Christ limited His phrases to seven during His most important hours of ministry on that first Good Friday. His cross said it all. And in silence, the cross on our flap communicates that same love and presence of Christ crucified in the midst of any given tragedy or challenge. Somehow, Christ's presence through our presence, brings redemption when nothing else can.

Dear heavenly Father, we are Your hands, feet and mouths as we continue to carry on the ministry of spiritual healing through the blessed Gospel of Christ's atonement. May we, Your children, be an encouraging presence to one another, especially when we feel weak, downtrodden and dismayed, to the glory of Your holy name. Amen.

AUGUST 28

IT WAS SIXTY-FIVE DEGREES Celsius today! August is definitely the hottest month. One day, the temperature was literally off the scale. I have a photo of a thermometer in which the mercury level surpasses all the indicated measurements. You need to drink water every twenty minutes, usually spiked with Gatorade powder or Camel Back tablets in order to help your body retain the liquid. Otherwise, you are sweating or urinating out fluid faster than you are drinking it in. The heat of Afghanistan gives a whole new meaning to the necessity of water for life. Here, I sweat like never before. When you have an extra seventy pounds of equipment on you, while on patrol for instance, you resemble a swimmer who has just climbed out of a swimming pool with his clothes on. You are soaking wet with sweat. This is ironic when considering that we are in the middle of some of the driest deserts of the world. Jesus Christ offers His disciples the water of life in a desert very similar, and not that far away from this one (John 4:5-14). It is an appropriate image and comparison. Without water, we die. Without Him, we die. Uniquely, His water springs up to eternal life.

It's not easy for the locals to acquire potable water. The Canadian and NATO Forces have provided innumerable wells for communities. Yet Christ makes it easy. He offers the water of life as a gift, freely. It cost Him His life. He battled the flames of hell on the fortieth day of fasting food and water in the desert. He battled the devil one last time as He hung in the heat on the cross, even to the point where this God almighty enfleshed cries out for water: I am thirsty (John 19:28–29). He is thirsty for us; for us to receive that gift, and for our troops to have relief.

Father of glory, only the gift of Your Spirit quenches the thirst of man. Look in mercy on all the ways that Your Church seeks to bring the fountain of living water to the world and prosper the preaching of repentance and forgiveness; through Jesus the Water of Life, Amen.

SEPTEMBER 4

FOR THOSE WHO CAN not attend the ramp ceremonies on the KAF for our Canadian brothers-in-arms who are killed in battle, we try to recreate something similar on the FOBs where the deceased had been based or had friends. Not only does this function as a sign of respect, but it also allows our men and women the opportunity to grieve, even for a few moments, before returning to the battle field. For example, yesterday we lost some men in an IED explosion. Today, at a FOB, I created a tiny chapel in our dining tent with some cereal boxes on a table holding up pictures of the deceased, two tea lights positioned at both sides, and a soy sauce bottle holding a small local wild flower between them. I hung a Canadian flag on some clothes pins for the background. There were many tears shed as soldiers came through the canteen to pay their last respects. I felt a tear in my eye, even though I didn't know the two young men well at all. It recalled to me the time when Jesus wept at the death of Lazarus (John 11:35). Why did He weep? Jesus knew He was about to raise His good friend from the dead, so what caused Him so much grief? Perhaps it was because He was witness to the hopelessness of the other mourners around Him and their lack of faith in Himself as the Resurrection and the Life. Perhaps His tears were a reaction to the greater reality of sin, death, and the suffering of others. According to the context, it is clear that it was His love for the living, instead of a simple personal grief, that caused God's Son to shed those memorable tears in the midst of this death. Christ was incapable of condemning those who crucified Him, and were crucified with Him (Luke 23:34). Dare we say that His love prohibited Him from that judgement? He is Love, and can only love. He forgives them. At the same time, He says very little. His silence confirms their self-condemnation.

I said very little today in that make-shift chapel. It may be due to the fact that I am not as comfortable in the French language as I wish I was (since I was working with a Francophone group). Maybe I was being wiser than usual. I read Psalm 23, prayed the Our Father, and simply said, in my broken French, "We don't know why things like this happen, but God promises that He is with us" followed by Jesus' words, "There is no greater love than to lay your life down for your friends (John 15:13). You were their friends. We are His friends."

We thank and praise You Jesus for redeeming us from our selfishness, pride, and ignorance . . . in short, ourselves. Give us the humility and courage to boldly, yet gently, apply Your Law and Gospel to the life situations of those You bring into our lives, so that they too can know Your loving presence and receive Your merciful salvation. Amen.

SEPTEMBER 12

WHY DOESN'T GOD PERFORM miracles more frequently, and demonstrate grand interventions on earth? This question pops up a lot after critical incidents. I wonder the same thing. In those moments I need to ask myself why it is that I think that He should. Is He somehow obliged? Are we deserving? Is not our freedom one of our most precious moral commodities? Despite our arrogance, ignorance and pride, the Lord intervenes all over the place, by grace. If I were God I would have abandoned this planet a long time ago. As a matter of fact, I neglect it every time I fail to help another creature. Yet, as we learn from Christ's temptation in the wilderness, the miracles of Jesus are not simply acts of humanitarian compassion. They show us His identity. The physical aid is always of a secondary consequence. Consider the healing of the paralytic: "So that you may believe that the Son of Man has authority to forgive sins . . . get up and walk." Otherwise, why not just keep people from falling ill, if Jesus were simply concerned for their physical well being? After all, even the resurrected Lazarus dies again.

Russian author Fyodor Dostoevsky's *The Brothers Karamazov* does a magnificent job revealing the enormity of Satan's infamous temptations for the Son of Man. Jesus was not tempted to prove His divine identity because He felt upstaged by the devil. He was tempted to help humanity, but in the wrong ways and at the wrong times. The devil's arguments were reasonable. They were ingenious as they touched Jesus precisely in the inmost depths of His heart and His love for us. "Jesus, think of all the good you could do if you turned these stones into bread. You could solve world hunger. Jesus, you want people to believe in you right? Well, jump down from this tower and they will see the angels lift you away. Jesus, I will give you all the kingdoms of the world. You would make the best king, leading the nations in justice and peace." It must have torn His heart declining those offers, and for what? Death on a bloody cross. By rejecting the offer, Jesus appears less than compassionate. By choosing to die, He appears less than sane. Jesus wants to help people. But the greatest help He can offer is eternal. A temporary solution to all the world's problems can actually have the opposite spiritual effect. As Jesus' casting of demons into the pigs demonstrates, sometimes even those who believe His claims and witness His miracles, chase Him and want nothing to do with Him. In short, miracles don't create faith, and, despite popular opinion, faith is more important than anything else on earth.

This all gives me great courage as a chaplain. When God appears absent and doesn't grant us that much sought miracle, I know that there must be a good reason, since I am sure that the temptation to intervene consumes Him more than I could ever imagine, due to His love for us. He is not a masochist nor is He a sadomasochist. The temptation to intervene is just as great as it was during those 40 days in the desert. Although resurrected and ascended, Christ still bears His wounds. He still suffers, as He sees us here, and hears our complaints caused by unbelief. But for me as a chaplain, I no longer try defending God when I find myself intervening in the midst of tragedy, not because I am disappointed, but because I love Him too much to make excuses. May God prevent me from offering those well intended, but hopelessly erroneous, explanations that simplify the tragedies of others. Job's friends were well-intentioned as well. They attempted to defend God's reputation, and were rebuked by the Lord. Instead, may I save my thoughts, and my words, for some heartfelt moans and groans as I drop to my knees in prayer.

Could it be that *I* am that miracle and "intervention," sent by God as His messenger and bearer of Good News? Forgive me Lord for the times that I believe otherwise.

Dear God, the world can be confusing at times, and we are often tempted to rely upon our own wisdom and reasoning to make sense of it all. Thank You Lord for the innumerable times that You forgive my errors which are driven by simple lack of faith in Your omnipotence and sovereignty. I praise You Christ for your patient commitment to using me as the answer to the prayer of others. Amen.

SEPTEMBER 16

IT IS A BIZARRE feeling to fall onto your stomach on a cafeteria floor along with close to 500 others. When the alarm is sounded and we hear "rocket attack" or "ground attack," that is precisely the procedure. Wherever you are on KAF, you drop down and cover your face. The voice, blasted over speakers throughout our base, occupied by close to 60 000 troops, reminds me of something out of an Orwellian novel. Out on the FOBs, there are no warnings before a rocket strikes, except for a short whistle about half a second prior. On KAF, it is unlikely that we will get injured or killed because the base is so large, though we have taken casualties from time to time. Often, by the time we hear the alarm, the rocket has already landed somewhere. We tend to get a lot more at the airfield, since the insurgents know well that that is where most of our fuel is kept. Lucky for us, their aim is lousy and they lack equipment. The rockets are usually set on an angle between some rocks. They are constructed of whatever combustible material is available to them, and catapulted from the mountains or fields. They have hit a couple of aircraft and some of our hangars. Immediately after an attack, every member needs to notify their CoC regarding their whereabouts to assure that everyone is accounted for on base.

We have had some close calls, and everyone knows it. The chaplain's take on things gets a greater hearing in times like that. More than a few have reconnected with God, or have started attending chapel or Bible Study. Hopefully those patterns persist back home after the tour.

Peace and security: we take it for granted. However, even at home, tragic surprises occur. Wherever there is sin, there is violence. It is inescapable. Even if I isolate myself in a desert, I cannot escape from the violence hidden in the depths of my heart. "Trust in the Lord." We don't have a lot of choice!

Almighty God, defender of the poor and weak, guard and protect us from the attacks of our enemies, of both body and soul, through Christ our Lord, Amen.

SEPTEMBER 18

SOME CHILDREN WERE SEEN with wire cutters, openly cutting the barbed wire that surrounds our FOBs. It is not surprising. We have here just another episode of insurgents sending their children to do their dirty work. The insurgents have periodically taken children along on their missions. Although some soldiers consider children in these regions as "potential terrorists" or "Taliban in training", most Westerners have a soft spot in our hearts for children. The enemy is well aware that we won't shoot at or deliberately kill kids, and so they play on our compassion. They have a lot of faith in our mercy. As I wrote a few days ago, we have a similar temptation with Jesus in the desert, where the devil tempts Him to stay on earth to satisfy all of humankind's temporal needs; an attempt at dissuading Him from going to the cross to provide for their eternal ones. Even the devil plays on the kindheartedness of God. And when we should, we don't. If only we had that same faith in our approach to God. We could move mountains (Mark 11:23), the Scriptures say. He too has a "soft spot" for children, which is why Jesus calls us His children (I John 3:1). And yet, we often prefer to wallow in our guilt or pride rather than putting our trust in His mercy, appealing to the compassion of one who has an impeccable reputation for kindness and fairness . . . as did the Taliban.

Lord, I believe, yet help my unbelief (Mark 9:24) when the tragedies of life cloud a godly vision of Your divine mercy and compassion. When my feelings and emotions mislead me, fix the cross of Christ before my eyes as the only reliable anchor of my faith. Amen.

SEPTEMBER 28

MY DAYS ARE EITHER incredibly busy, or amazingly quiet. What is God teaching me? Even when I am surrounded by crisis, it is not always evident what my role is, or how to respond. In the Canadian Forces, responsibilities that were once a chaplain's have been shifted to other mental health care professions: social workers, deployment support centers, etc. Perhaps due to the trends of specialization in our society, which tend to fragment communities, our trade has been transformed. Perhaps the military has tried to alleviate our heavy work load by dividing up the tasks. Or perhaps it is simply a case of pushing aside the religious figures in hopes of rendering them obsolete. But, whatever the case, the question that rests in the back of my mind, whether I am responding to trauma on a busy day or contemplating life on a slow one, concerns my role as a chaplain. When do I assert myself more, or pull away and say nothing? When do I handle the situation myself, or refer it to a "specialist"? When do I manage the problem myself or bring in other members of the team? I am sure that I don't get it right even half the time. It is a good thing that nobody has complained . . . yet.

But chaplain presence proclaims a divine presence. It, by definition, must be an awkward presence. This isn't always a bad thing. It awakens awkward feelings in the hearts of many with whom we have contact. My ongoing attempts to justify my role, by often trying too hard to demonstrate my importance, reflect my own insecurities. Instead, I should simply be satisfied to be there and ready for . . . whatever happens. I recall Elijah's experience with God who wasn't in the center of the action: not in the fire, nor in the storm, nor in the earthquake (I Kings 19:1-18). Rather, He was found in the *whisper*. Are we not echoes of that whisper as chaplains? How hard it is, though, to be that whisper, deliberately off to the side, passed by and unnoticed by all the busy bodies, some of which undoubtedly think you are in the way. Others seriously wish that they could slide into your trade so they can shoot the breeze over a coffee with their friends, since that's all they think that you do anyway.

Like Martha attempting to imitate Mary after their encounter with the Lord of rest, it takes all my energy to, well, do nothing. Salvation is, after all, about doing nothing. We can't work for our salvation. Ironically, it is hard work to achieve rest. It is not easy entering into that *receiving* zone in contrast with the *serving* mode. Yet salvation often comes in those moments of whisper. The whisper is that which is heard by ears who make it their goal to listen, and are thus impacted by what they hear. Everyone hears the fire, storm, or earthquake, and are perhaps terrified or overwhelmed. But listening to a whisper requires deliberation, persistence, even concentration. Hearing is not listening. Listening requires an active intention.

At times we are the listener to the voice of God. We need to focus our attention on His word and wisdom. At other times, it is we who channel that voice as a care giver. There, too, we implement a deliberate act of caring about what we are doing or trying to say. Sloppy and unfocused talk is the noise of a wind, fire or earthquake. But a word of comfort, the Gospel applied in just the right place at just the right time, is the whisper of the heavenly Voice. There is no need for a chaplain to feel guilty standing off to the side, waiting for just the right moment . . .

Have mercy on me, Oh Lord, a poor miserable sinner. Forgive me for underestimating Your ability to use me as Your instrument, particularly when I feel and believe in my worth the least. In Christ Jesus, Amen.

OCTOBER 3

SOMETIMES WE CHAPLAINS NEED to travel by foot to visit the troops, because they are not accessible by vehicle. This can resemble a foot patrol.
The logistics are identical. The risks are the same. It is an eerie feeling
when you walk through the flour-like dust of an Afghan desert in the full
knowledge that your next step could blow you into pieces. It is common
knowledge that IEDs are planted all over our AO, and are our most dangerous menace. Sometimes dozens of soldiers will step in the exact same
spot before it blows off under some unfortunate young man's foot. You
walk by faith, trusting that your next step will not be your last . . . even
though it could very well be!

When we consider the question of walking by faith versus by sight
(II Corinthians 5:7), the world tends to see "religious people" as irrespon-
sible and childish for placing the greatest value on faith. This is in spite of
the fact that all human activity revolves around faith. Even secular philos-
ophers such as Wittgenstein have convincingly argued (against their own
materialism!) that one can never be absolutely certain about anything in
life. Instead, we consider some things more probable than others. I have
faith that when I walk out the door there will be a floor underneath my
feet. I believe it is so because every time I have taken that exact same step,
there has been floor under me. But why is it that I believe that there will
be a floor the next time? My belief is based on my past experiences, but
there is no guarantee that I will experience the same thing in the future,
during my next step. We all live by faith. The dispute depends on the reli-
ability of the object of our faith.

Consider the moon. From earth, we can never see the moon. We
only observe the reflection of light off of the moon. In fact, we never *see*
any objects at all, but simply are exposed to the particles of light that they
reflect. In this respect, faith is "as solid" as sight. Perhaps we could even
say that we are closest to the object, and able to see that reality best, in the
dark! What a strange thought. For what is faith but trust? For the Christian, it is holding onto the promises of God in the darkness. I trust that
Christ walks with me on patrol. And even when the mine does explode in
my path and under my feet, it explodes with Christ right there beside me.
And He takes me to that place where no mine can ever again harm one of
His dearly beloved children.

Lord, walk with me in those moments of darkness, and be my Light and Life. Increase our faith in Your leadership, until we enter the Kingdom of Glory, through Christ our great Guide, Amen.

OCTOBER 8

MINES: OUR GREATEST ENEMY. Today we lost 2 engineers from an IED strike, and a couple others were wounded, including an officer friend of mine who lost the lower part of his face, some fingers and a knee cap. I had a chance to visit with the rest of their section after the event, to help the members decompress and facilitate their grief. The sergeant in charge was filled with such guilt. It was not his fault, and yet there was nothing that I could say to bring him comfort. Why is it that we often feel that we need to say something, instead of nothing? Probably, it represents an attempt to ease our own awkwardness, and, in the case of a chaplain, validate our presence. So I made the mistake of trying to explain that the enemy was to blame, but to little avail. However, I refused to forget this faithful leader. At the end of my time at that FOB, I found a cook and gave him a cross that I had made out of two sticks of wood and a bit of string, and asked him to pass it on to that sergeant. I myself was unable to track him down. I have no idea the impact of that gesture: whether he would be insulted or grateful; angry or moved to tears. Regardless, the message of the cross transcends any of our mixed emotions. It will, one day, give him the consolation that he desperately requires. It offers us an invitation to cast our burdens upon the One who so patiently hung upon two sticks of wood.

Lord Jesus the Crucified One, You alone bring hope and comfort to heavy hearts and consciences. Forgive us our sins of both commission and omission and free us from our prisons of guilt. Amen.

OCTOBER 13

RECENTLY WE HAVE BEEN on a high level of security alert due to an abnormally large number of rocket attacks from the Taliban. The enemy plants Chinese rockets targeting our FOBs. As a timer, they use plastic pop bottles filled with water. When the evaporating water from the desert heat reaches a certain point, it crosses two wires triggering an electric charge, firing off the rocket. Since the rockets are balanced on field rocks, their aim is terrible and, although they are set up not far from us, normally they miss us entirely, although some explosions have been within 200 meters. Yet sometimes, *albeit* rarely, they get lucky. One happened to land in our midst at about noon yesterday. I heard the squeal, which gives you just enough time to duck your head, and saw a huge explosion not far from me, followed by a cloud of toxic smoke in the sky. There are many squeals throughout the day. Those who work the artillery fire canons whose blasts will literally knock you off your feet. Then there are the IED explosions or "thumps," depending on their proximity, and bullets gone wild from a gunfire episode. Incoming rockets give off a slightly different sound. Anyway, when I ran to the scene I saw a huge sea container with a six foot hole in its side and a truck on fire. Apparently, the door was open and the rocket passed through it, broke through the opposite wall and hit part of the engine, popping four tires. I learned afterwards that two mechanics were under that truck just a few minutes prior, but decided to grab lunch early that day. As they were walking away the rocket struck. Thankfully, all the dangerous shrapnel was confined in the container and truck.

On another occasion, a rocket landed on a Canadian shelter burning it down. Thanks be to God that no one was in it at the time, and the damage was isolated except for some rips in nearby tents. In both incidents (and, there are not enough pages in this journal to record all the stories of similar "close calls"), the soldiers told me that they were "lucky," whereas I asserted that they were "blessed." There is a difference. Although we cannot know why bad things happen to one person and not another, it is good to give thanks to God for all the times, both big and small, that He rescues us from danger. We are equally sinners and we all deserve the worst that life can throw at us. But why some get off easier than others is beyond our understanding. We can say with certainty that if God wasn't with us, things would be a lot worse. Do we really understand grace if we make comparisons between ourselves and those that have it better, or worse, than us?

Another spiritual lesson learned is that we ought never get too angry when we are late for an appointment, miss the bus, or get caught up at work. We may even curse God for the unforeseen delays. But who knows what your life would have looked like if everything was on schedule. Perhaps God held you back those few minutes, in the office, or permitted that crisis to occur at the last minute, just to keep you off the road, due to an inevitable car accident that awaited you. Of course, you will never know. But the angels of God do. And I believe that they act on our behalf, in every time of need, which is probably a lot more frequent than we would like to imagine or are prepared to believe.

Lord of the heavenly hosts, I thank You for the angels that deliver to us Your help and rescue, directing the eyes of our hearts to the great salvation achieved by Your dear Son, our Lord. Amen.

OCTOBER 19

THIS MORNING AT 0430 I woke up to assist with a ramp ceremony. As I stood there beside the Hercules aeroplane listening to the prayers as the coffin was loaded on, I watched the sun rise over the desert hills behind the heads of the line of soldiers before me. There was complete silence as the body advanced towards us. The sun resurrects, and so does hope. There are very few moments in a soldier's day in which he or she abides in silence. In silence, one is forced to reflect upon that very silence. Silence either consoles or terrifies. It is always uncomfortable. We are not at ease with silence. Even believers commence their nervous coughs during those lengthy moments of silence in a church service, when those private prayers or confessions are to be lifted to God in the quiet of our hearts. The silence always has a purpose. If it is only to awaken that sense of awkwardness in our inner beings, it is well placed. Silence makes us more resilient, because it reminds us that we are not in control of our emotions or of our destiny, both in the next few seconds or the years ahead. Someone else is in control: the pastor who decides to react to the cough, shortening the silence with his intervening words; the pall bearers who decide to speed up the pace to shorten the awkward moment. And then there is God. I believe that Jesus was often silent. I think that perhaps this is one reason why He loved St. John so much. John, we could say, was the silent apostle. He listened a lot, reflected even more. He was all the more faithful, courageous and compassionate because of it. There was only one disciple who chose to find himself at the foot of Christ's cross, despite all the risks to his own safety. That was John. May we, likewise, imitate his way. May our soldiers imitate ours.

Father of Lights, whose mercies are new to us every morning, teach me to listen to Your Gospel voice and remind me of the importance of silence both in giving to others and in receiving from You; through Jesus Christ our Lord. Amen.

OCTOBER 24

APPARENTLY MARTIN LUTHER ONCE said, "I am so busy I only have time to pray." As a Lutheran theologian, I love such paradoxical syllogisms. This one is intended to prioritize prayer. Prayer changes not the heart of God, but rather the heart of the one who prays. God does not need our prayers, but we ourselves need to pray. Certainly God has already answered many of the prayers that we should have prayed, but didn't. In short, He is full of grace and cares for us despite our own neglect. However, as Luther said elsewhere, God has a treasure chest full of jewels that He is just waiting to give to us. He is simply waiting for someone to ask. Well, here in Afghanistan, I have more time to pray than I do at home. There, after the busy work day, errands and children take up most of my evenings and weekends. By the time night time comes, my daily prayers have become my family prayers. The bed time devotion routine, which is absolutely invaluable and I miss it dearly, cannot replace that daily quiet time that every Christian ought to have with their Lord, even if it be only five minutes.

Here, on the other side of the world, I have no family and few errands to complete. My laundry is done for me, my meals are cooked for me, and my bunk takes about 10 minutes to clean. My work week follows the track of a roller coaster. I am either really busy or really bored. Nevertheless, most of the time, I can easily find time to pray. Besides noise, there is not a lot to distract me from this spiritual discipline, and so, sad to say, I do it when I have nothing else to do. I realize that it is a bit like giving God the leftovers instead of the first fruits. But our Lord and King is so kind and humble in heart, that He even takes the crumbs, and happily at that. Did not the Gentile woman in the Gospel reflect that heart of God when she boldly spoke, "Yes Lord, but even the dogs take the crumbs from the master's table" (Matthew 15:27)—and so was praised? Is not the Gospel about God coming down to serve us, undeserving as we are, and save us? Is that dynamic different now after the resurrection and ascension of Christ, or does He continue to operate in the same way through the divine liturgy and sacraments? These are some of the wondrous jewels that I have discovered in the repentance over my neglect of a healthy prayer life. What a remarkable God we have! The lessons learned in our sinfulness are as precious as those learned in saintliness.

Our Father who art in heaven, who gives us a Spirit that "prays without ceasing" (I Thessalonians 5:17), teach me to value the gift of prayer and come to You often in petition and praise, not as a burdensome task and work of the Law, but as a liberating privilege and celebration of the Gospel; through our Great High Priest, Jesus Christ, who intercedes for us always before the heavenly courts, Amen.

OCTOBER 31

As a chaplain serving in the Roman Catholic context of French Canada, amongst cultural Catholics whose worldviews often maintain the worst elements of religion, sometimes I get the feeling that soldiers take me as a superstitious lucky charm. I compare myself to a rabbit foot. From an operational perspective, the CoC is supportive of whatever stabilizes the guys to help them get their jobs done. If a chaplain's presence achieves that, then all the better. I remember once leaving a FOB for a few days and after returning, one soldier said to me, "Padre, all hell broke lose when you were gone," while another insisted that there were "more contacts and firing than usual." In reality, the level of threat had not changed a bit. Rather, their perception was that, when the priest leaves, so does God. Accordingly, they were more sensitive to a spiritual isolation and vulnerability during my absence. At first I was slightly offended by the idea. As a Lutheran I am opposed to superstition, views of an impersonal God, and any doctrine inculcating a soteriological hierarchy expressing divine favouritism among people. However, after some further reflection, it offends me less. The superstition that underpins their desire for a chaplain with them impressed upon me the importance and the impact of chaplain, or pastoral presence, amongst the troops. Although the majority would not consider themselves religious, they hold on tightly to a belief that we really do carry something significant and unique. On some level, these superstitious and "spiritually immature" soldiers understand that God is "tabernacling" among them (John 1:14). When they ask me to bless their rings, chains or other trinkets, I use it as an opportunity to educate them about the living God. Would I like each one to believe that they too can possess the Holy Spirit, be a tent of our compassionate God, and acknowledge a priesthood that allows them equal access to the holy things of God? Absolutely. But we all need to start somewhere. And, furthermore, it usually takes a prophet to make a priest.

Jehovah God, our Mighty Fortress, on this Day of the Lutheran Reformation, I praise You for the advancement of the Gospel around the world through missionaries, pastors and chaplains. May each and every Christian boldly proclaim Your saving Word to those among whom they are asked to "tabernacle;" through our Rock and Redeemer Christ the Lord, Amen.

NOVEMBER 8

I MET AN AFGHAN Christian today. He saw my cross and greeted me with, "*Salaam Alaikum.*" Discovering that I was a Christian pastor, he got excited and began telling me all about his Bible. I asked him if he ever attended the chapel. "Yes I did, sir . . . one time. But never again. People noticed me." This is not the first time I have encountered a "secret" Arab Christian, one who risks his life daily for his faith and convictions. They have so little, yet are willing to give it all up for Christ, when it would be so much more convenient to simply adopt the religion of their infancy and go along with the national flow. I don't actively seek them out, but I am easily found. I am publicly a Christian chaplain. I usually speak a word of encouragement, and keep them in my private prayers. "We will meet again on the other side," I tell them. I admire their commitment and boldness. And then there are us Canadians . . . sigh. We habitually complain about church services interrupting our precious Sunday schedules. And meanwhile, here are our brethren, who would, literally, *die* to get to church. Many have, are presently and will continue to be counted amongst the martyrs. Jesus promises. What a mighty testimony against our own religious apathy. We are so quick to give up the most precious treasure imaginable. And it takes a poor third-world Afghan to remind us, simply through his identity, of our misplaced priorities. He is rich in Christ, and he knows it, which makes him both wiser and wealthier than all the rest of us in the "developed" world.

> *Dear Lord, You are the help of the helpless. Thank you for the martyrs of the church and the example that they have set for us. Forgive us Christians in the Western world for storing up treasures on earth, so that we too may be a living witness and powerful testimony of the priceless treasures of heaven; through Christ our King, Amen.*

NOVEMBER 10

IT IS CRITICAL THAT chaplains be viewed by our troops as "value added" military personnel as opposed to simply priests wearing a uniform. Otherwise we can easily be viewed as a "waste of rations" by those who do not understand our trade. When others do not appreciate or understand our role, the doors through which we minister to them become locked tight. I noticed that today when I helped identify a possible IED through some binoculars from a guard post. This soldier on sentry duty was impressed and word gets out fast. Another time I remember spending only one hour helping unload cargo with a couple of guys; just lending a neighbourly hand. Yet it made the world of difference to my ministry amongst them. Despite their ignorance regarding the details of my job description, they were convinced that it was better that I was there that day than not. Earning the troops' respect is the first step to moving "into the loop" and into their lives. When others think that you have something useful *to do*, they are convinced that you may have something useful *to say*.

> *Holy Spirit, make me an instrument of Your holy peace in both word and deed, so others can partake in Your divine healing; in Jesus' precious name, Amen.*

NOVEMBER 11

JUST A FEW HOURS ago, I had to carry a cadaver to a drop zone, through a labyrinth of compound walls. My partner left immediately after we completed the task, and I found myself alone. It was dark and all I had was a small pen light attached to a button hole. To my dismay, I couldn't find my way back. All the mud walls look identical. Then I looked at my boots and the ground beneath my feet, and I saw black droplets that had marked the sand. The blood had been dripping from the corpse, conveniently providing me a path to follow back. I could not resist the temptation of recalling the story of Hansel and Gretel. Strangely, it got me to thinking about Jesus. I couldn't help envisaging my Lord after His beatings and scourging, dripping blood all along the way to Mount Calvary. I envisaged the soldiers following Him as the very ones who would later pierce Him. Jesus, who is the Way, provides the way; a pathway marked by His innocent and precious blood. And there were the soldiers following their Savior and they didn't even realize it. After all, it was a Roman soldier, an infantry man, a strong macho independent-type likely, who first confessed that Jesus was the Son of God (Matthew 27:54). Immediately after Jesus drew His last breath, and before viewing any subsequent miracles, this soldier confesses how this butchered piece of meat strapped on a tree, is God. What made him come to that conclusion? The crucifixion appeared to be the ultimate failure for the Christian. "If you are the Son of God, come down from the cross!" (Mark 15:22) the other soldiers shouted. But this particular soldier heard Christ's words, and began following His trail of blood all the way to the heavenly kingdom. Are we not that soldier, following the same blood trail, every day? It doesn't express a life of glory, but does offer us a heavenly home. "Today you will be with me in paradise" (Luke 23:43), is a daily promise of God's patient presence for those who believe. As was the case with that Roman soldier, faith cannot help but to respond with, "truly this man *is* the Son of God."

Christ my Leader, may You continue to abide with me as I travel on the narrow road towards heaven, a pathway marked by Your own atoning Blood. Amen.

NOVEMBER 16

TODAY ON THE MUSLIM festival *Ede* we received a mass casualty at the ROLE 3 hospital, resulting in minor injuries to our soldiers: shrapnel wounds and amputated fingers. Two young children on their way to the market to buy new shoes for their religious festivities experienced more severe injuries. The cause: a suicide bomber strapped to a donkey! This was a first! It was the butt of many a joke in the evening updates: "suicide donkey." Even the wounded Canadians blushed in embarrassment. If the insurgents would only channel their creative energy into more productive places, their skills would open up an unthinkable horizon of entrepreneurial endeavours. The sad reality is that these extremist Muslims, fighting this war in the name of religion, lack respect for their own holy days. In fairness, it could have been caused by mercenaries from Pakistan and elsewhere, explaining the constant battle rhythm even during the season of *Ramadan*, a pattern that was absent during the first few years of the mission. These individuals tend to have less religious convictions. But in this case, the donkey rider was an old local man, who probably saw those children playing in the street every day for years.

Was it worth it? Really? I mean, even during WWI, there are stories of armies halting the battle in order to celebrate Christmas together. However, the extremist versions of Islam reveals a foundation in fear. In fact, suicide bombers are cowards, not courageous. The only assurance they have of a direct entrance into heaven is through this kind of violent act. Otherwise, it is anyone's guess whether or not Allah deems a particular follower worthy enough for his holy company. In short, self-sacrifice in exterminating the "white devil" is the surest and, in fact, easiest way to heaven, even if it does result in the death of fellow Islamic children. I do not claim to be objective. But I am grateful that my Faith teaches the notion of justification by grace. God gladly invites all who trust in Him into His holy presence, without reason for fear. Certainly, without Christ's atonement, there is definitely plenty of reason to fear God's holiness and righteous judgement, due to His redeeming sacrifice on the cross, we have an assured place in heaven.

It would be unfair to claim that all Muslims hold to the view that Allah is unpredictable in his judgements, and the Koran does use "Gracious One" as one of the many names attributed to God, but among the *Pashtun* Afghans a culture of fear is perpetuated by Islamic extremism.

Accordingly, education is targeted. The Taliban consider the notion of a secular school system as inconceivable. The most prestigious schools in Pakistan and Afghanistan are the *Madrassas* which are notorious for indoctrinating children in the ways of radical Islam and recruiting the strongest and brightest for religious leadership. Some have referred to them as "factories for *jihad*," usually funded by rich Saudi Sheiks. From our perspective, basic education involves teaching people how to clean a wounded finger to avoid inevitable infection and amputation. Yet the local medical doctors are barely familiar with the basics of antibiotics. As it stands, children avoid schools, because they are targeted as Western sympathizers and, thus, enemies of pure Islam. Why is education such a threat? Education instills criticism and demands change. Even if that change simply calls for the use of a clean bandage as opposed to a dirty piece of linen. Iran had its own political and cultural struggles due to its highly educated, and thus, critical population. The leadership has chosen to manage them by a show of force. It resembles Europe, and the power structures in place by the Pope prior to the protestant Reformation. It is no coincidence that the Reformation would never have survived had it not only been for the invention of the printing press to better facilitate the spread of its principles, but also the perpetuation of mass literacy and education. In short, the Taliban are correct in their assessment that cultural adjustments are coupled with political and economic reforms. And, of course, the religious ideas will follow. In a theocracy, amongst an uneducated and easily persuaded people group, the argument for our elimination from Afghanistan is a strong one. Consequently, I wish that our leadership would pay careful attention to our witness in that country; that we do our best to fit into *their* culture. Canada has a particularly good reputation for being respectful of other cultures, but at the same time, the kinds of magazines we read, TV shows that we watch, food that we eat, etc. has already had its effect on the population here. Once I went to great lengths explaining to some Afghans that not all Canadians are fans of the sport of women's wrestling. Female soldiers and clean shaven non-bearded men insult the average Afghan. More importantly, they fear changes to the only culture that they know. With or without intent, from the very first contact with a new culture, both cultures are changed slightly. We need to be extra-sensitive and deliberate in the delicate case of rebuilding Afghanistan. Not every country celebrates multiculturalism and diversity. Democracy is itself a kind of culture. The question is, can it be incorporated into, or will it corrupt, the Afghan kind? The answer to that question will determine the longevity of the war and the strength of the insurgency.

Returning to the subject of the Canadian casualties: I was able to re-assure them that their sacrifice was not in vain; they are truly heroes. The "donkey bomber" was on his way to explode himself at a Canadian compound with various unarmed civilian media present. They stopped him, by their bodies. As Christ has redeemed us from hell and all its hordes, so our faithful men and women of the Canadian Forces bravely redeem their fellow brothers and sisters.

We praise you Lord Almighty for the sacrifices made by our soldiers in battle overseas: a reflection of the greatest of all sacrifices made by Your beloved Son in the war zone of Calvary. In His precious name we pray, Amen.

NOVEMBER 17

I USED TO THINK that chaplains were the most important people for the morale of the troops. At least that's what they tell us at Basic Training. I have since learned otherwise. The chefs are. The way to a man's heart is, after all, through his stomach. The challenge for the chaplain is to create that same hunger for spiritual food. So here's a little trick: we make sure that we are present serving supper at the kitchen, at least a couple of times a week. Not only does this allow people to get to know your face, and you theirs, but it also allows you to be associated with a positive experience (as opposed to seeing you at the hospital because of an injury or in your office because of a crisis, for example). For this same reason, during death notifications, a commanding officer will normally give the bad news, instead of the chaplain, to avoid the longer term association of the padre with those difficult words. Subconsciously, the family will be more hesitant to receive comfort and care from the bad-news bearer. The padre sticks around for the aftermath. After the CO departs the house, the chaplain may be asked to stay anywhere between several hours or days. Often a prayer is offered and certainly comforting words of the promises of God are conveyed.

It is not always possible, but we try to disassociate ourselves from negative experiences, so that the member can receive care from a neutral zone. Symbolically, this is expressed on the parade square, in which the padre has no designated place. Instead, he or she stands off to the side, despite his or her rank as an officer. It is a visual depiction to the soldier that the chaplain is, in many respects, outside of the chain of command. When soldiers come to see me, I usually treat our meetings together as a confession, and will inform no one else nor implicate others without the consent of the member. There are some exceptions to this, of course, such as when the member poses a threat to him or herself or another. This is rare. In the other health care trades, the counsellors do not necessarily possess that privilege of keeping information to themselves. They are often obligated to write up every intervention. Contrariwise, we chaplains do our best to be the safe zone, a sanctuary, so to speak. We can be compared to the temple in the Old Testament. Does this mean that we always fight for the interests of the member? By no means. This is especially the case in war time when the interests of the unit and the operation take priority. A soldier may feel entitled to return home briefly for the funeral of a good friend. Intuitively, this may seem reasonable. However, his absence means that there is one less soldier on the ground. His platoon becomes less safe. Furthermore, accommodating his request on a compassionate basis sets a precedent for others undergoing similar circumstances. Many factors need to be taken into consideration before a final decision is made. The member is not normally aware of what goes on behind the scenes after a request to act on his or her behalf has been made. Regardless of the outcome, that soldier needs to know that there is someone, a friend, on the outside and the inside, who can be there for him or her in whatever trial he or she undergoes. This is a role of a chaplain. Even if I don't sympathize with the request, and will make recommendations contrary to it, I still consider it a privilege to have been approached by that member, since God and my country have appointed me to serve him or her. Appreciating the sanctity of my vocation hopefully allows me to maintain a pastoral spirit despite the circumstances.

Back to the topic of food. Two weeks ago we prepared supper for 500 people with one BBQ! I never cooked so much in my life. What a fun and great opportunity to serve our troops a meal. As one chef told me, "we crown each soldier king . . . each meal ought to be fit for a king, since it could be their last."

Lord of the Church, we bless You for the mission to which You have entrusted us, Your baptized children, of extending Your healing grace so that others may join Your holy fold; through Christ our Lord, Amen.

NOVEMBER 18

ONCE AGAIN, I PULL out my blue surgical gloves in preparation for the arrival of some wounded or dead. Although I am trained in combat first aid, there are usually enough medics around to do the work. I don't particularly enjoy hanging around corpses. I am there to be close to the troops and it is appreciated. My presence is a support to them. I become one of them, just as God became one of us. As St. Paul wisely points out, we are to be "all things to all people" (I Corinthians 9:22). Christ has provided us the most perfect of examples in His own life and ministry of presence amongst His people. And so I offer a hand wherever I can: helping the kitchen staff as they clean the grease or restock the freezers, taking a turn at cleaning the toilets which are often soiled by the Afghans who are accustomed to squat, moving ammo with the engineers to lighten their burden, or sweeping the floor and emptying the garbage. There are limits however. Once on a convoy a driver put a machine gun in front of me. I told him that chaplains are not permitted to fire arms. Some Canadians are uncomfortable with the mix of metaphors: priests with guns. He said, "There's the safety switch, just in case." Although that platoon was shorthanded, my hands were tied.

As an officer, some of these tasks may seem beneath me; but as a chaplain, they are right up my alley and demonstrate my trade as one of service. The washing of feet happens in unique and peculiar circumstances. The fact that we chaplains are not hesitant to get our hands dirty is noticed and respected. Once a soldier remarked on my taking out his trash. I responded that this was, in a way, symbolic of my ministry. People come to me with all their problems and brokenness, and I carry it out for them. And where do I take it? To the trash hill of Golgotha where Christ burns it away forevermore with His redeeming sacrifice on the cross.

Lord God our Faithful Friend, teach us to serve others with the attitude of our Savior, who served us throughout His life and ministry, culminating in His Passion and death; through the same Jesus Christ we pray, Amen.

NOVEMBER 19

I WAS ASKED TO give a devotion for the coalition chaplains today before one of our weekly presentations. Here are my notes:

"Come to me all you who are weary and heaven laden, and I will give you rest . . . For my yoke is easy and my burden is light" *(Matthew 11: 28–29).*

At Ramp Ceremonies, I always enjoy looking at the different stoles or preaching scarves worn by the chaplains from all different nations. For many nations, these mark us as chaplains, but do our troops know what they signify? Do we? The stole represents the yoke of a donkey: its burdens. As clergy others give to us their burdens through confession, discussion, prayer requests, stories, etc., and after a while that yoke can feel heavy. Sometimes it results in what mental health specialists call "compassion fatigue."

What ought we to do with these burdens in order to protect our own peace of mind? Well a good priest is a mediator between the divine and the human, and he is expected to transfer that load to God through Christ. But why, in practice, do we have such a hard time doing that? Is it because we do not trust God with the burden, although He alone is trustworthy? Is it that we perceive ourselves as strong and capable of carrying it alone, although the Scriptures tell us that we are all, by nature, spiritually weak? Does it represent an unconscious engagement into our own self-therapy, which circumvents the great physician? Is it due to the fact that we ourselves want the praise, rather than allowing God to have that glory? Perhaps, it is a little bit of each. Nevertheless, it is essential that we give the burden up. Otherwise we become less effective in our ministry. Furthermore, it is sin not to. To which command is it contrary, when we refuse to give our burdens to the Lord? Here we have a neat spin on the question. It is contrary to the seventh commandment, according to the historic numbering. In other words, essentially, withholding the burdens of others is a kind of theft. They do not belong to us, but rather are the possessions of Christ, who purchased and won them by His holy and innocent Blood shed on the cross. He bought our burdens, and exchanged them with a light one. So let us let Him have them!

A pastor friend once conveyed to me how he never "gets anything in the ministry right." For instance, he delivers the comfort of the Gospel when he should preach the demands of the Law; or he preaches Law to an already guilty conscience which requires the immediate consolation of the Gospel. He is never comfortable in his role as a pastor. But isn't that as it should be? We do not represent ourselves as ministers. God used a donkey to preach to Balaam, typological, I believe, of the holy Office of the Ministry. We are walking examples of weakness and brokenness, so that God's power and healing can be manifested in and through us. Yet let us not add to this image, by carrying an unnecessary load. For the load that the Lord has laid upon us should suffice as a reminder of our true identity.

NOVEMBER 21

THIS MAY SOUND GROTESQUE and sadistic, but I search for opportunities to be with the dead; whether they be the corpses of the local Afghans, insurgent Taliban, or our own Canadian or American brothers and sisters in arms. It's a good way to both observe and support the young Canadian guards, many of whom have never seen a body bag. Their only exposure to the horrors of death and dying have been by television and computers. But when you see the real thing, for the first time, it can be a real shock. If you haven't yet noticed, death is deliberately covered up in Western society. It is contrary to the American dream: "become whatever you want in life." For instance, it has become increasingly unpopular in North American society to take our children to funerals, or hospitals, lest we expose them to these "negative" environments. "Positive energy" is hard to come by amongst the dying.

This all contributes, of course, to a less resilient population. Many Canadians have a harder time dealing with stress and trauma when they are older because they have been so carefully protected from it while they were young. My grandfather fought in WWII, was captured by the Russians and spent a decade in a POW camp. Did he have PTSD? Who knows—probably, a bit. He used to snap in anger whenever he saw us kids playing with toy guns. He suffered horribly during the war. I know that this took a mental toll. Yet nobody talked about it as out of the ordinary, and, somehow, the family got by. Poverty and tragedy were a regular part of life back then. People were accustomed to losing a child before their adolescence due to some medical condition, easily curable today. In short, they were, well, to put it bluntly, stronger. Today, we hide it. Women apply makeup in attempts to look younger. Men colour their hair and mimic the behaviors of the younger generations. We lie about our age, and joke about being x number of years "young" instead of "old." Instead of being proud of our experience and acquired wisdom over time, we glorify youth, and become a less mature society because of it. The *Pashtuns* may have all sorts of social problems, but they get this one thing right. They respect their elderly. It is not shameful to be old. It is honourable. The Bible describes it as a blessed state. And death, then, is a natural transition into eternity. *Pashtuns* fear death less. Perhaps this is one of the greatest weapons of the enemy: they are patient (since they have so little, they have all the time in the world to cause mischief). They also have nothing to lose. Pain may be a punishment, but not death. Death is often perceived as a gift; an escape from this world into the next. One doctor explained to me how on one occasion a man brought his crippled son to him, in order to have him put to sleep: a mercy killing. He was, after all, of little use on the farm and a drain on financial resources. The father was not a monster. He was not simply a practical man, either. He loved his son, but death was not the worst case scenario. Worse still was living handicapped amongst the various physical, social and psychological elements of Afghanistan. Of course, the doctor declined the request, but the event will never escape his memory. Stories like this haunt us. But for the *Pashtun*, there is no shame in death.

I figure that jobs working with the dead are a great challenge for soldiers, and so my presence with them injects a kind of comfort and even sanctification to their vocation. In practice, it means that I help move corpses from time to time. The Afghan Taliban corpses are normally evacuated to KAF for investigation, and I would often be asked to carry them to, and load them onto, the choppers. I am there anyways, so I may as well make myself useful. Contrariwise, the corpses of the other civilian Afghans were handed over to the Afghan authorities. This means that we simply carry them to a graveyard next to the Afghan compound attached to our own. Our Canadian soldiers work closely with the Afghan army and police, acting as mentors to them in being more effective in their trades. (During my second tour to Afghanistan I see remarkable improvements in the level of professionalism amongst the Afghan National Army, in comparison with the first. The local populations trust them more because of it.) The bodies, when lacking any identification, are left in a hole a couple of feet deep. A stick with a piece of cloth wrapped to the end marks the grave. The Afghan burial rites are simple. The deceased are delivered into the hands of Allah and forgotten forever from the minds of men. The Afghans remain curious about our practices regarding the dead. They love to observe the care that we take with the deceased, and the various religious practices that surround them. Frequently the Afghan commander, who is also responsible for the spiritual welfare of his troops, has invited me for lunch. The discussion will at some point climax in questions of Christian funeral rites. Even the most secular Canadian soldier expects some sort of prayer or moment of silence at a ramp ceremony.

The Judea-Christian custom of treating the cadaver with great care is rooted in a belief in the redemption of the body and soul; a visual expression of the belief in the physical resurrection of the dead to an eternal life in a physical new heaven and earth. Muslims respect this, while, at the same time, their own theological system arguably has roots in ascetic and Gnostic sects. Before criticizing the Afghan burial practices too severely, it is paramount that we realize that, to them, we look rather vain. For them, once the member dies, they no longer belong to us humans, but have become the possession of the company of heaven. They believe that those persons live on in the afterlife, and, so, why place great importance on the body in the here and now? After all, funerals are intended to aid the grief of the living and not the dead. The deceased receive a new identity with God. Accordingly, no tombstones or naming of any kind appear at an Afghan grave. It remains an unmarked hole in the earth. The corpse is placed therein, on its side, and facing Mecca. A short prayer may be said. However, no family members are encouraged to visit the place of burial thereafter. When I was working in the hospital on KAF, the Coalition Forces expected some sort of short religious service prior to the transfer of the corpse to the Morgue. Normally, this ought to be conducted by a Muslim, and the only ones qualified were the Afghan interpreters. It would frustrate me at first to see the lack of priority they placed on helping me prepare the body for movement. I was often stuck there alone with one of *their* corpses. I would read a psalm, wrap the body, and face it towards Mecca. In retrospect, I think that I judged them too harshly. After all, five minutes translating a discussion between an American nurse and a wounded Afghan is much more appreciated and valuable than five minutes with a padre and a corpse.

For the Afghans, death is such a common phenomenon among the living that it is a luxury to concern oneself with the dead. After all, time and money spent on the dead necessitates less time sustaining the life of the living. For this reason, when a child is injured, a grandfather will arrive at the hospital in order to provide care, since the father has other duties, and women are not permitted a public role. At the same time, the Afghans do not altogether dismiss burial rites, and are horrified by the rumors that, in the West, Christians have begun burning their dead just like the Hindus! In an age where cremation has become the more popular means of disposing of the deceased, often because vain Westerners do not like the idea of their bodies rotting in the ground (ironically, they would rather be set aflame while their bones are crushed into small pieces) the military still exhibits traces of the historical Christian burial rites. An impressive amount of respect is demonstrated towards the body of a deceased member of the Canadian Forces. Even in KAF, at the Morgue, a Canadian will never be stored with the body of a deceased insurgent. When only pieces of the body remain, they are handled with great care by our troops and Mortuary Affairs. After the visitations and Ramp Ceremony in KAF, they are flown back home for another Ramp Ceremony in Canada, after which they are escorted by convoy on the highway to the member's home town. The financial costs of the funeral are all covered by the Queen. Families appreciate the deep respect exhibited by the Canadian Forces for our fallen comrades.

Once, when a fallen soldier was not flown directly to Trenton, Ontario, but passed through Ottawa in order to drop or pick up a VIP, the family was outraged that the aircraft had been obliged to stop. Well, it is just an empty shell, isn't it? What's the big deal? Well it may be an empty shell, but it isn't *just* an empty shell. The body is, according to the Christian worldview, a belief system that still underpins many of the military's traditions, a sacred vessel of God. One cannot have a proper view of the incarnation or the sacraments, if cremation is preferred over burial. Hindus burn the body in order to free the soul from this evil casing. In Christ, God assumes our humanity thereby purifying the things of the earth. The consecrated elements of bread and wine are nothing short of the ongoing manifestation of this sacred union. The divine and human are attached . . . forever. The beauty of the body and all of creation is restored.

I am not asserting that those who are cremated find no rest in heaven. But our acts reflect our theology. If the army asked if they could use your dead grandparent's body for target practice, and then give it back to you for burial, would you agree? Certainly not. Ridiculous? Indeed. We intuitively know that the body is more than just flesh. Perhaps we know, deep down, that the body is the temple of the Holy Spirit, and that, even when our spirit departs, it is still somehow a sacred tabernacle. In any case, it is made by God, and our God does not endorse that sort of destruction. If something is broken, you don't break it into more pieces. You either fix it, or dispose of it in a proper manner. Cremation, somehow, breaks it down even more. At least that is my "traditionalist" and humble opinion on the matter, and it appears that millions of people in the Middle East would agree with me.

Faithful keeper of every promise, Your Son has told us that whoever believes and lives in Him shall never die. With joy we thank You for those who live in Him, though their bodies rest in the earth. Bring us to the unspeakable joys that they know in Your nearer presence, and help us to never lose hope. Amen.

NOVEMBER 25

HERE I AM, WAITING for a lift out of a FOB, by a heavily armed Chinook helicopter, which functions as a kind of air bus to take personnel from one FOB to the next. The wait can sometimes be delayed anywhere from a couple of hours to a couple of days. But it is a lot safer than the convoys, which are always at risk of hitting some IED on the way. That being said, the choppers also get shot at with small arms and RPGs from time to time. No matter how fast we clear the area, and despite the numerous cameras we have in the sky, attached to balloons, towers and aeroplanes, the enemies still manage to bury their mines in some creative and unusual locations. The question is whether the ones that our vehicles hit will cause injury or death. I am waiting at the landing zone and covered from the heat which is, I kid you not, about 50 degrees Celsius presently. I am in a concrete containment cell which formerly held Afghan POWs waiting to be transferred out to KAF for investigation and detainment. While I lay here on a an old rusty bunk peering through the metal bars at the mountains beyond, I hear an IED go off, or it could have been a rocket landing, followed by gunfire. About 30 seconds prior to the explosion, the Mullah started crying his prayers from the local minaret situated about 500 meters from the corner of where I am. The minaret has a reputation for being used by insurgents to spy and fire upon us. Our SOPs prevent us from firing back, especially at a Mosque. Imagine the media coverage. Reporters would have a field day spin doctoring the news that the Canadian infantry attacked a sacred Mosque. Plus there is the collateral damage, and we pick up the bill. Now, most Afghans are friendly to our Forces, but we are in Zangabad, in the South of Afghanistan. This is Taliban country. As far as we know the Mullah is shouting out tactical commands. What a bizarre mix of sounds: the chants of prayers and the blasting of bullets.

It is not uncommon that the military leaders are also the religious leaders. In fact, whenever some chaplains go OTW, they take off their flaps marked by a cross. Any faithful Taliban would assume that the chaplain is the commanding officer, due to the Taliban's theocratic principle which intrinsically unites the realms of religion and politics. But things were not that different in the Western world before the Reformation. The inquisition was founded upon a similar confusion. It began with Constantine of whom St. Augustine was highly critical. The *City of God* distinguishes the difference between the kingdom of earth and the kingdom of heaven, condemning their confusion as demonic. It was Luther who clarified the idea of, for lack of a better expression, "the separation of church and state." In short, theological battles are to be fought not with metallic swords but rather with those of the Spirit through religious dialogues and discourse. Spiritual battles are not of this world. While the Roman Catholics and most of the Protestant groups fought out their differences through physical violence, the Lutherans had an outstanding reputation for keeping those worlds apart. I am quickly reminded that those lines continue to be crossed in another time while presently being fired upon by Taliban insurgents from the minaret of a Mosque. Thankfully, in both worlds, in both kingdoms, God gets the final word. Regarding my immediate predicament, I live in the hopeful expectation that my life rests between the secure and merciful hands of Almighty God. Eschatologically, it means that Jesus does not simply return at the end of the age in order to bring spiritual peace, but to end all temporal wars as well. Our Scriptures assert that heaven will involve both a spiritual and physical rest. What a different world awaits those of us who hope.

O God, from whom come all holy desires, all good counsels, and all just works, give to us, Your servants, that peace which the world cannot give, that our hearts may be set to obey Your commandments and that we, being defended from the fear of our enemies, may live in peace and quietness; through Jesus Christ our Lord, Amen.

NOVEMBER 27

A CAPTAIN FRIEND OF mine was injured a few weeks ago and repatriated back to Canada. He was quite the athlete, good looking and exhibited the most positive attitude, but his life will sadly never be the same. His face is unrecognizable, and his young children are still trying to familiarize themselves with his hideous appearance. The captain had come to see me before the patrol, and with the typical queries of a "seeker" posed the question, "Why does a loving God allow tragedy?" The fact that there is a name for the study of this question (i.e. theodicy) should remind us that our contributions on the topic are rarely original. In the Book of Job, which is one of the oldest Hebraic Scriptures, the subject is openly broached. And, of course, God is the author. We forget that sometimes. It made my friend think. After a long discussion on sin and grace, he expressed his intention to come to church. Unfortunately it never happened, due to last minute scheduling. There was another time that I wanted to pray for him before a patrol that we went on together. He wasn't comfortable, because he didn't want to alarm the other men of the level of danger. Ironically, it was this same patrol, two weeks later, that resulted in damage to his face. Not surprisingly, when I saw him in the hospital after my tour was completed, he was very open to praying with me.

Consider the amazing lengths to which God goes to in order to bring us back to Himself, to repentance, which is synonymous with "turning." God has no delight in suffering, but it is often the only way to break through the proud walls of our stubborn hearts and have us turn to Him. Naturally, a child thinks that the discipline that he or she suffers hurts him or her more than it hurts the parents. As a father I believe that the reverse is true. When I discipline one of my children, it is usually with less force than a playful tap. In other words I am more physical with them when we play! So it is the humiliation that really stings them and makes them cry. As a result, I often find myself in deep pain witnessing them in pain. Even though it is they who are responsible for it, I am still somehow a cause, according to Aristotle. I inflict, or "cause" the punishment, and cannot help but to feel somehow guilty. After all, it is my hand that carries out the verdict. Of course, my children usually forget about it all after thirty minutes or so, but I remember it for days thereafter. I have no regrets. Both justice and responsible parenting require that we discipline our children. And, again, though their sin is the cause, it is hard not to think that I too am somehow responsible. They are flesh of my flesh and bone of my bone. I love them as I love myself. And yet I know only a fraction of love, as my heart remains selfish and darker than the depths of the ocean. But God, our heavenly Father *is* love, and He only wants the best for us His children. When He disciplines us, I suspect that He hurts infinitely more than I do over my kids. His sacrifices are endless and constant. Still He considers it worth the pain, so that He can have us with Him for eternity. And in light of the length of eternity, and the price that He paid, how could anyone disagree?

> *I thank you my heavenly Father, through Jesus Christ Your dear Son, that You have graciously kept me this day; and I pray that You forgive me all the sins that I have done wrong, and graciously keep me this night. For into Your hands I commend myself, my body and soul and all things. Let Your holy angel be with me, that the evil foe may have no power over me. Amen.*

NOVEMBER 29

Violent sand storms, poisonous scorpions and spiders the size of a baseball: "we aren't in Kansas anymore," as Dorothy observed upon her arrival to the land of Oz. Even the insects are aggressive in this apparently God-forsaken land. Between attacking ants and the most courageous and hungry mice that I have ever encountered, it sometimes feels like we have crossed over from earth to the border of hell. Even Genghis Khan regretted his journey through this harsh and stubborn land. "Padre, it's too hot here for even the devil," one soldier commented. That being said, it is not too hot for God, who is shockingly familiar with abiding in the evil places of the universe. So this land is not forsaken.

But truly, poverty is the greatest of this country's woes. There is something to be learned about Christianity's effect on culture. The most admirable parts of Western culture are derived from the influence of the Church, despite the fact that most people today take for granted our public hospitals, justice system, charters, constitutions, governmental charity, etc. Without trying to sound ethnocentric, societies where the logic and compassion of the Gospel were lacking evolved differently. For instance, the Christian notion of the priesthood of all believers underlined the fact that God loves all equally and has no favorites (James 2:1-13). This doctrine brought Europe out of the dark ages and into the modern age. She was transformed through the empowerment of the individual conscience and celebration of the humanities. Equal status before God led to mass public education, literacy, and the notion of equal rights among people. In most expressions of Islam, we find nothing similar to this. Women and children have little value. Women are useful for producing children, cooking the meals, and being mules for their groceries, but not much more. Children are potentially useful when they achieve adulthood. Amongst some Afghan clans, little boys are useful for other unspeakable tasks, in accordance with the *halekon* tradition, but little girls are safe, due to their gender and sexual "uncleanliness." In *Pashtun* culture women are necessary for child birth, but undesirable for pleasure. At least paedophilia is technically illegal in Afghanistan, which is a step in the right direction, and reflects a willingness and openness to change the negative characteristics of the culture. In a sense, changing Afghanistan requires a changing of worldview, one that is more aligned to the *best qualities* of our own, since we ourselves have much to be ashamed of as well. (In British Columbia we have groups of educated citizens seeking the legalization of paedophilia!) Accordingly, many Muslims are afraid of our influence upon their culture. The people-groups which inhabit the southern part of Afghanistan have consistently been opposed to rule from the Northern and more "civilized" regions of Afghanistan, as well as the presence of foreign forces, whether they be British, Russian, or NATO. The mere fact that we are present, restricting and surveying their daily routines in search of insurgent activity, restricts their local autonomy and independence—key principles of their culture and religion. We are considered "*kaffir*," an evil pagan and polytheistic influence on their culture—a culture which they believe to be divinely established. The vicious cycle of Western hate is only perpetuated by our efforts at trying to minimize it. A war of *Jihad* is not optional for them. It is demanded. In such a theocracy, any change in culture carries a religious implication. And so, in a sense, one could argue that the conflict in Afghanistan, if understood in a certain way, is a religious war . . . on both sides.

Almighty, everlasting God, through Your only Son, our blessed Lord, You commanded us to love our enemies and to pray for those who persecute us. Therefore, we earnestly implore You that by Your gracious working our enemies may be led to true repentance, may

have the same love toward us as we have toward them, and be
of one accord, and of one mind and heart with us and with Your
whole Church; through Jesus Christ our Lord, Amen.

NOVEMBER 30

TODAY WE RECEIVED A mass casualty and, strangely, children were brought in. Normally children are not prioritized by their own people, and it is not uncommon for the women and children to be left to die after an incident. However, these two children had a father whose love surpassed these cultural norms. The wounded little boy smiled at me with a great big grin framed with crusty blood spread on to his forehead and stitched up slashes on his chin and cheeks. He was a CAT C, which means, in short, that he'll be alright. I can't help but imagine the face of one of my three boys instead of his own. I empathize with the father. Yet what on earth was the boy smiling about? He doesn't *have* anything to be happy about, or does he? He's just happy to be alive for another day. He's happy to be cared for. He's happy to be loved. No wonder Christ loved the little children so much. How open they all are to reciprocity. How easy they are to please and convince. A smile back goes a long way. When an adult man does the same thing at home in the city he is regarded with suspicion. Distrust is of the world of adults, but trust belongs to the universe of children. How easily they believe and place their faith in a stranger. God is no stranger, and yet we second-guess Him constantly. "Unless you have faith like a child you will never enter the kingdom of God" (Matthew 18:3). Despite our adult-like ways, thank God He still considers us His children.

Savior, grant us faith to believe that you are indeed the Conqueror
over sin, death and all evil forces, and that the battle is won and
the victory is ours, even when the evil one seeks to deceive us.
Amen.

DECEMBER 2

I KEEP A CERTAIN sermon tucked away in my clip board as a spare (in case of an emergency). It is an "object lesson," meaning that the preacher has a certain tangible object in mind that he can show to the congregation, which he uses to point people to Christ. No matter where I travel out here I am surrounded by one particular object that makes my task of preaching the Gospel rather simple. Every soldier has a ton of kit to wear: helmet, anti-fragment vest, webbing, etc. Well, at the end of the day, they need to put it somewhere. In order to keep it off the ground, our soldiers have constructed wooden crosses on stands, and leave them outside their sleeping quarters and work stations. In short, I am surrounded by crosses! I may see the cross, but our soldiers need a bit of help. My sermon revolves around the weight of sin and how Christ takes that burden onto Himself on the cross. I place one of these cross stands in front of me during the service. I begin the sermon with the kit strapped on my body, and by the end of the homily I have transferred it to the cross. Those who attend "get it" every time. My final words encourage them to think of how their burdens and sins are taken away by Jesus every time they see one of these crosses.

Sometimes I wonder if God predetermined the cross as the method of achieving our salvation, because images of crosses are all around us. The Polish artist, William Kurelek loved painting the landscapes of the prairies of Saskatchewan. But if you look carefully at many of his canvasses you are bound to find a cross with an image of Jesus barely visible. For instance, there is one in which a row of telephone poles are depicted in the foreground. Off to the side, a Christ figure hangs with his back towards the viewer, with only the top of his head and knees exposed. Jesus hangs there watching a family having a barbeque and going about the daily mundane routine. Jesus watches over us, silently and patiently. Crosses are everywhere. The reminders are plentiful, for those who seek them.

King of kings and Lord of all, may Your arms of forgiveness, that were once stretched out upon the cross, continue to extend to all nations, even in the midst of war and strife, welcoming the repentant and embracing the contrite. Amen.

DECEMBER 3

IF YOU STAND OUTSIDE the medical tent long enough, you are sure to witness a jeep race around the corner of the sand-bag wall of our FOB, carrying a load of human remains. Sometimes the victims are the injured; sometimes they are dead; sometimes they are both mixed up together . . . with their pieces. Without getting into unnecessary detail of casualty scenes that I would rather forget, it strikes me how strong people are when they are dying. Consider the adrenaline factor: that push to live in the midst of certain death. The Taliban have a little help. Some are "self medicated," that is, they are stoned on opium before they get injured. Maybe they should be rewarded for being proactive. I have seen more than one of them die with a smile on their face while missing more than one of their limbs! It is hard to sympathize or respect people in that condition. I feel sorry for them, in so far as this is the only life they have ever known. They are unable to criticize their own cultural underpinnings. They are young and easily influenced. The real Taliban, however, are the educated Arabs who live in palaces, far away from the battle field. Yet the *Pashtun* thugs resemble child-like gangsters: a disorganized band of tyrannical bullies. They are not all that scary looking nor are they physically strong. Their sole advantage over us is that they are patient. They have all the time in the world to sabotage our work, and place little value on their own, often miserable, lives. Many are simply waiting for the day when NATO forces entirely withdraw out of Afghanistan. Then they will attempt to regain control.

I believe in our mission here, and wish that we would stay longer. We in the West are far less patient than they are: fast food, fast fix, fast war. Still, whether or not these criminals deserve our medical aid, our doctors fight for their lives. Doctors refuse to let the enemy die without doing everything in their power to keep them alive, even against their own will to be treated by an *infidel*. Our med techs and doctors are often exposed to the violent threats of the patient, who prefer death rather than suffer the shame of imprisonment (or should we say, the shame of being imprisoned since our detention cells are a four star hotel in comparison to their own accommodations). I remember one man who had lost the lower half of his body, and the medical team, with their best efforts, continued to do all they could to stop the bleeding. He cursed the staff until his last breath, according to the interpreter.

Jesus Christ, incarnate Word, You became flesh and dwelt among us, even while we were Your enemies. Empower us by Your Divine Spirit to, likewise, love and serve our enemies; that we may offer them hope in this world and peace in the next. Amen.

DECEMBER 5

"WHY DOES THIS AFGHAN soldier keep asking if I am a Father?" I ask. "Padre, he heard there was a priest around, and wants to know if it is you. He has been a Christian for 15 years, in secret, and has been begging to see the priest since we arrived here." That is how this morning began. I could justify meeting with him because, although he was one of our most trustworthy national workers, he was driving the other soldiers crazy. This way he would stop harassing the Canadians with his urgent demand. Of course we would have to meet in private. I couldn't invite a "terp" (i.e. an interpreter) to join us either. It would be too risky. We met and communicated by means of a white board. I prayed for him. He didn't know what I was saying, but it didn't really matter. Although an interpretation of this peculiar instant of *glossolalia* would have been welcomed, he was simply grateful to find himself in the presence of another Christian. The lengths and risks he took just to be present with other Christians are remarkable! Even the rumor of his Christian status could result in his execution. And we, in North America, are too lazy to get up for church. We leave the church because the lady in the kitchen said something insulting. Christian fellowship is a gift from God. This Afghan soldier longed for it. And even when we have irreconcilable differences, we learn to live with one another, and show love towards one another. In heaven, after all, we will spend eternity with these people that we do not like . . . in love. So God begins His training of us on earth. To skip a scheduled training in the army is a chargeable offence. Repeated offences could result in eventual dismissal. God deals with us in a similar manner. As a great theologian once said "you can't say `Lord, Lord I love you, I love you . . . but your wife is fat and ugly.'" If you love Jesus, you love His church as well. If you are found in His Body, well, low and behold, there are others there too! You are not alone. In fact, they may be as uncomfortable with you as you are with them.

When I was a civilian pastor serving in the parish I preferred offering Holy Communion with the large cup as opposed to the small individual ones. We are, after all, one large cup as the Church, as opposed to a series of small individual cups (and not disposable!) on a platter. We are not a series of individual bodies, but one Body: one vine, one bread, one church. A love of the body is a love of self and expresses a love of the head, Christ. I must learn to love and accommodate the other parts, as they keep learning to love and accommodate me, since, after all, these are the people with whom I will spend eternity.

Heavenly Father, Your Son knew hunger in the wilderness and yet His reliance on You never failed. Give to Your baptized people, amidst the many temptations that they face in this age, trust in Your promises and hope in Your final deliverance; in Christ, Amen.

DECEMBER 6

THE STRENGTH OF TRIBAL ties in Afghanistan is shocking to us in North America who have a hard enough time simply keeping our families together. On the down side, faithfulness to the clan is often at the expense of the good of others. For instance, there are guides who have discouraged us from sweeping out mines in certain districts because they do not benefit their own people. They care little for the safety and welfare of their fellow country men, as their allegiance extends only to their own tribe. It is common for locals to make false reports about their neighbours hiding weapons on their property, as an attempt to carry out a tribal feud that has been on-going for decades or even centuries. Jealous *Pashtun* Afghans who have worked on a project with us one month, may be found attacking us the next month, simply because we have given the next contract away to someone outside of their particular tribe. Wealth is too precious to share.

Although as a Canadian I am horrified by this sort of behavior, I need to remember that these people live in a desperate circumstance. And when desperate, everyone, including us Canadians, would find ourselves doing shocking things, all in the name of survival: survival of the family; survival of the tribe. A tribe is none other than a people group with a distinct culture and history. The moment that we realize that the maplines of Afghanistan, Pakistan, and India are artificial, that tribal identities surpass geographic boundaries, we begin to understand why it is so difficult to "conquer" Afghanistan. Imagine a country made up of countries. And then visualize these countries overlapping each other. The wars between the tribes are even more vicious than that between our Coalition Forces and the Taliban. To some tribes, we are perceived as useful in advancing their interests. After all, they will remain here forever, while our presence is temporary. We are *all* well aware of that. I am not suggesting that our work here is in vain—quite to the contrary. Progress has been made. Infrastructure has advanced. Attitudes have changed. The impacts are permanent. The fruits will eventually become visible, in the next generation of Afghans. If only we were as patient as they!

God of wisdom, amidst the cruelty, chaos and irrationality in this world, I ask that You enlighten the minds of leaders to rule with justice, carry out their duties with reason and serve their subjects with humility, advancing the cause of peace in this land; through Christ our Lord, Amen.

DECEMBER 8

Before I get too upset that I am often the last to know or be informed of details and tasks that require my aid or presence as a chaplain, (such as being omitted from the invitation to medals parades, which, consequently, I frequently miss; or when the medical liaison forgets to call me from the hospital informing me of those less-severe causalities whom, consequently, I visit too late) I need to remember the striking similarities between my trade and God's trade. Both of them demand human faithfulness, of which all of us earthlings are incapable. For example, although He is preoccupied with me all the time, I come to Him last with my concerns. I am always on His mind, and yet He is one of my afterthoughts. He is often the last with whom I share the goings on in my life. Of course, because of His omniscience, He already knows everything before it happens. But He would still like to hear it from me. God knows our prayers before we pray, and yet He still asks us to bow our heads and fold our hands. When I "skype" my family, my wife often answers the phone/computer and gives me updates on recent events in the lives of my kids. But this never precludes me from asking them to describe those experiences to me in their own words. I am insulted when they neglect to tell me, even though I already know the answers. It is a parental instinct.

Communication reflects a relationship of trust. Through communication, we are brought into the circle, and into the world of the other. Without it, we are on the outside . . . a stranger. I wish never be estranged from my children, as God desires never to be estranged from us.

Welcoming God, Your Son's embrace of the outcast was limitless.
Break down all the barriers that would keep us from sharing Your
acceptance and love with others and help us to treasure and value
each person as one who is precious to You through Your Son's
sacrifice; through Jesus our brother, friend and Lord, Amen.

DECEMBER 10

WE HAD JUST BEGUN a new operation, and one of our Chinook helicopters crashed due to an RPG launched by insurgents. At least that is one claim. This same unit lost two men last year when one of our Griffons went down. Without downplaying the pilots' impressive landing, it is truly a miracle that everyone escaped safe and sound, and remained uninjured, even while under enemy ground fire. Everyone agrees that it is absolutely amazing . . . a helicopter crash without any injuries to the two dozen people on board! Shortly after evacuation, this huge monster of an aircraft was caught up in flames, and was reduced to a metallic ball of scrap metal. We received the message at KAF that we had Mass Casualties coming into Medical. Everyone waited in anxiety, expecting a parade of stretchers from the Med Vac choppers. Instead, the passengers all walked off the runway towards us, in peace. Everyone agrees that it was a miracle.

Luther wrote about the power of prayer; about how even just a few Christians praying for something can change the world. We chaplains pray daily for our units. Of course, many attribute such incidents as described above to chance. However, their prejudice does not preclude our gracious God's interventions on our behalf, even to those who despise and ignore Him. How many people's lives have been changed due to the prayers of others, and they remain unaware? I wonder. God knows. We may not think about God all the time, but He is definitely all-consumed with us . . . each one of us . . . all the time. And He shows it, in both the big divine interventions and the small miracles that happen every day in each of our lives.

Lover of Humankind, You send Your Gospel into all the world that
people might be delivered from the power of the evil one. Pour out
Your Spirit continually on all military Chaplains, that they might
proclaim Your Word truthfully and with boldness; through Christ
our Shepherd. Amen.

DECEMBER 11

DESPITE POPULAR OPINION IN some evangelical circles, we pastors are not here to teach people how to live, but how to die. I do not simply mean dying to self, in terms of Christian repentance and confession, but also physically. We all need to ready ourselves for our entrance to the grave. As one Protestant Reformer once said, "The moment we are born, we begin to die." This view is not pessimistic, nor does it implicate a "kill joy" approach to life in general. It produces a reality check. It is a reminder of our mortality and our pilgrimage towards our real and secure home. To die to self means to live in Christ. Thinking about dying changes the way we live. It makes us more generous with our belongings, for they will not remain with us for long. It moves us to be more liberal in time spent in service and even prayers spoken for others. Our focus is directed towards the other. It even acts as a survival technique. Last night an American brother in Christ shared with me how he felt the first time that he was shot at during his first tour in Iraq. He was a sentry in a tower. He froze for what felt to him like minutes, but was likely only seconds, before he dropped down for cover. After that, he learned from his friends that the only way to live in war is to pretend that you are already dead. This is the only way to gain the necessary strength to face the enemy. In the end, death is our greatest enemy. To face it we must confront it. Jesus Christ has conquered death on our behalf, but we still must pass through the gate by ourselves, even for a short moment. When we accept our identity as dead, we can rejoice in our hidden identity as alive together with God in Christ. It remains concealed to our human experience, but is ever more revealed by faith.

Some military organizations prefer not to use the word "death" in briefing new soldiers and their families for deployment. They replace the idea with other expressions such as "if something happens." As for my experience in such matters, I have yet to encounter a soldier or his wife scold me at the utterance of that taboo word during our chaplain pre-deployment briefings. Many have expressed sighs of relief after hearing the chaplain levelling with them and articulating in an honest manner that undeniable possibility that everyone is already thinking about. By trying to tip toe around the elephant in the room, the CoC loses credibility amongst its people. "If you can't trust a chaplain, who can you trust?" I hear that a lot after a member confides something in me. Well, we are in the business of death, for the better or for the worse. By confronting our fear, we conquer our fear. If being up front about death was our only task as a chaplain, it would validate our presence a million times over.

Provident God, teach us to live not by our eyes, experiences and even our hearts, but rather by faith in Your everlasting and never failing promises; in Christ, in whom all Your promises are "yes" (II Corinthians 1:20-22). Amen.

DECEMBER 13

"WHAT'S HIS NAME SERGEANT?" I ask. "Corporal Smith, padre," he replies. "No, I mean his *first* name!" I respond. That is not the first time this dialogue has occured within the CoC. I realize the reasons why we do not use first names. Individualism can jeopardize our mission. Military uniforms are identical in order to express anonymity. We are, after all, a machine. However, one of the privileges held by chaplains is that we are at liberty to speak to the members as individuals. Their personal problems or physical wounds are, after all, not shared by the rest of the team. Soldiers have a number, but their person cannot be reduced to a number. They have a name. God calls us sheep. Sheep all look the same to some, but not to the shepherd, especially to the Good Shepherd. This is an appropriate metaphor for another reason. Here in the pastures, sheep often have more value than people. Was this the case back in the days of Christ? Is this perhaps why He has called us His sheep? It makes no difference, really. We are precious to him, because we belong to Him. We are treated as individuals and not simply as a flock. How often have eyes lightened up, coupled by a puzzled look on the face of a new recruit, the moment an officer addresses him or her with their first name? The wound is unique so the method of care is unique. All of it corresponds to a name that is unique.

Another privilege with which we chaplains have been entrusted is that we are able to become the rank of the other whenever we are counselling. We become the equals of our clients. We are not required to "look up" while advising a Colonel on his personal life, and, God forbid, that we "look down" on that Private who has come to see us with his drinking problem. Rank requires inequality, but we address those who come to us on their own turf and on neutral terrain. As Christ, who was far above the angels, did not consider equality with them as something to be grasped (Philippians 2:6), but became one with us, we chaplains follow in those very footsteps and in that humble tradition. We chaplains keep that human element afloat. What the military needs to hear time and again, is that the human element is invaluable to the sustenance of the machine. Without sounding overly utilitarian, the machine functions better when each of its individual parts, no matter how tiny, receive proper care.

Eternal God, source of light and life, may we who are chaplains always be deeply conscious of Your abiding presence and our responsibilities to care for Your people in combat. Deliver us from all error, pride and prejudice and make us considerate of those with whom we serve and those entrusted to our care. Instill within us courage, integrity and compassion and the desire to seek and do Your will in this great ministry. In Christ, Amen.

DECEMBER 14

I KNOW THAT IT is a strange question, but why do we find it so difficult to look upon the dismembered body parts of a fellow human being? Here in the desert, after looking after a body bag for an hour, you start thinking crazy thoughts. But there is usually something sensible underlying those confused thought processes that arise in unnatural and bizarre circumstances. These thoughts poke at our primordial instincts. One of my responsibilities is to minimize the exposure of the young soldiers who shoot the enemy, to the dead and wounded bodies of the enemy. Otherwise, there is a greater likelihood for a soldier to undergo PTSD. The first wounded Afghan to whom I was exposed was missing all of his arms and legs, and his face. Surprisingly, he was still breathing . . . for about twenty minutes. After many months, my memory retains an image of a rectangular block of red meat on a stained stretcher with two plastic tubes protruding out the top. An image that occasionally manifests itself in my dreams. Censorship works. Images are powerful. Hiding the blood and gore is not always practical, since these same soldiers are often asked to help the medical team, guard a dead Taliban before the body has been properly inspected, or clean up the mess afterwards. In short, I get to see their facial and verbal reactions at every step in the process. At first, before reaching the desensitized stage, they are often horrified. I wish I was more horrified, which concerns me sometimes.

Anyways, we eat animal meat, and often see dismembered animals at butcher stores or farms. So why are we so repulsed by a human body? Can it simply be explained by some sort of psychological predisposition, or is there a deeper spiritual reason at play? A Christian may argue that it is due to the fact that the human body uniquely contains a soul, created in the image of God Himself. Accordingly, we have an innate respect for the body because of its relationship with the soul. The Gnostics would disagree, due to their fundamental belief in the juxtaposition of body and soul. However, I believe that the body is, although fallen in sin, still a holy vessel. Both soul and body have been created in the image of our Creator, which is why, although the incarnation was the greatest of all miracles, it shouldn't be totally surprising to us Christians. The body is intended for eternity. Adam and Eve were not supposed to die. A limb detached from its body is simply not normal nor godly, and thus disturbs our primordial spirit. It shocks the inner part of our being. When it doesn't, we have ceased being completely human, which is why, incidentally, I tell our soldiers that they are mandated to kill, but to pay careful attention that they never begin enjoying it! This can be difficult in our present age of violent video games. The moment you love killing a fellow human being is the moment you have begun to compromise your humanity.

The body of anyone, enemy or friend, is created in the image of God. We are all equal in birth and in death. We remain brothers and sisters in life. War and killing are necessary evils, but our reaction to those evils is something that we can control. The moment our reaction becomes common and normal, the moment we are not alarmed by violence, becomes the moment that we have forgotten our divine origin. We sever the I-Thou relationship with the Divine and, in short, we cease to believe in God.

O God, in Your silence every anguished cry is heard; each person is created in Your image, all people are precious in Your sight. Receive into Your peace the victims of persecution and hear the lament of those who mourn their killing. Rid every heart of violence and vengeance, that hatred may be banished from the face of the earth and the family of nations brought together in peace. Grant this through Christ our Lord. Amen.

DECEMBER 15

"Be strong in the Lord and in the power of His might. Put on the whole armour of God, that you may be able to stand against the wiles of the devil. For we do not wrestle against flesh and blood, but against principalities, against powers, against the rulers of the darkness of this age, against spiritual hosts of wickedness in the heavenly places" (Ephesians 6:10–12) .

When I was a kid and I heard the verse above read in church, I always imagined the shiny, silvery, medieval suit of a knight. Ever since I joined the military, the verse has taken on a different meaning for me. The armor that we use today is rather different than that of the days of King Arthur. Regardless, it does the same job when we wear it, and the consequences are the same when we don't. The Canadian Forces, which has some of the best armor in the world, continues to improve and develop its armor. For instance, our anti-fragment vests have incredibly durable metal plates, and our protective eye wear has no competitor. Every year additions are made that cover more of the soldier's exposed body, while at the same time minimizing any impediments to his or her ability to move. Recently shoulder pads have been added, and we were issued throat protectors. I have seen with my own eyes the damage on the flesh when shrapnel or bullets strike an unprotected part of the body. And I have witnessed the remarkable difference armor has made to bodies that would, otherwise, remain totally vulnerable. Armor saves lives daily. And yet, how many souls stand naked, exposed to the weapons of the evil one and the companies of hell, while the full armor of God hangs off to the side, remaining in easy reach. The armor graciously provided in Holy Baptism gathers dust in the spiritual closets of our lives.

Our bases are surrounded by either 12 foot high concrete or sand walls, which are held together by thick paper and chicken wire. Believe it or not, they offer amazing protection from gun fire and rockets. Many lives have been saved by these impressive barriers. Life in KAF is a bit like living in a labyrinth at times, walking or driving through a jungle of concrete walls with little signage to show the way. Sometimes it even appears that it is over done . . . until the shrapnel of a rocket results in no casualties, thanks to all this armor.

The armor of God, the importance of Christian faith, may at times appear to be exaggerated by the Christian preacher or chaplain, until the emergencies strike. Those who lack the armor are left despairing. Personally, in the war zone, I find that more people gain faith than lose it. "There are no atheists in foxholes," goes an old saying from WWII. It is during the quiet and safe periods of life, that one becomes lazy in prayer. Slowly, as we look less and less to Christ, His Word leaks out of our hearts, resulting in an eventual loss of faith entirely. But in war, it is difficult to resist the temptation to think about God . . . whether you want to or not. You begin to recall those lessons learned in infancy. You at least wish or hope that there is a God that loves you.

As a preacher of the Good News, I count it a great privilege to serve our troops overseas. Certainly, it is at the expense of family. There are key events in the development of my children that I will never have the opportunity to witness. I will never see the first steps taken by my youngest child. There are experiences that my wife would have loved to share with me that will never happen again. We have all given up months and years of our lives in theater when we wished we had been home with friends and family doing other things. Moreover, I am different now. I live with a recurring nightmare in which my family is tragically killed by a plethora of disasters, and I stand by as an observer, unable to intervene. One night they are trapped outside the house during a hurricane, and I am locked inside, helplessly watching through a window. Another night they are trapped on a school bus with no functioning brakes, rolling down the steep road of a cliff, and I can't get in the door. I find that I am less trusting than before. I am more short-tempered and bossy than I used to be. I will never fully regain my former personality. I pray that my wife and children never resent me for it all. Christ has called us to despise our families in comparison with the love we ought to have for the message of the cross. I will have plenty of time with my family after my deployment, as I will after this common Christian mission on earth is over; when we enter the new heaven and new earth. Only then will the battle be over and the victory won. In the mean time, during this holy season of Advent, may we not become apathetic and forget to watch, and check our armor to assure that we are well equipped in our never ending battle with spiritual principalities.

God of the universe, You are our sword and shield as we wage war against the evils of the world, the flesh and the devil. May we, Your Christian soldiers, return daily to the waters of our Baptism to be rejuvenated and regenerated in this holy battle; through Christ our Captain, Amen.

DECEMBER 16

SOMETIMES I BECOME VERY much aware of the generation gap between these young soldiers and myself. This happens when I find myself wondering about how this unexpected experience of being with nineteen year-old teens and listening to swearing and dirty talk for hours on end, connects with all my years of Post-Secondary education! It is humbling sometimes, the menial tasks of an army chaplain. And how much of the same sorts of mundane duties did the Son of God suffer before His first public miracle? Most of His life is unrecorded, and was probably pretty uneventful. Almighty God incarnate, patiently living among us and with us in all our ordinary ways. It is incredible. St. John says that Christ did innumerable miracles that are not recorded in the Bible (John 20:30). But that was after His Baptism, at the age of thirty. Except for some apocryphal claims, which are dubious, I think that it is safe to assert that the young Messiah lived a pretty mundane uneventful life. Why would we expect something different for ourselves? However, one lesson that we can draw from the life of Christ is that the world can be changed by only a few isolated acts. We too change the world at given moments in our lives. Certainly we impact this world by the little things we do and say. But there are also those more significant events that trigger a greater change. Unlike Jesus, we may not be aware of the transforming waves caused by our actions. But when we get to heaven, we are allowed to ask. Then, if there is a movie, God may show us, and we will realize that what we thought was menial actually changed the world.

God of peace, You made peace with us through the atoning sacrifice of Your beloved Son our Savior. Thank you for making us your peacemakers and help us to persist in that blessed mission; in the name of Jesus, Amen.

DECEMBER 17

ONE THING I MISS during my deployment: reading the Bible with my family. My wife and I are raising our four kids with the practice of daily evening devotions. We simply read the Scriptures and teach them to memorize Luther's Small Catechism. It takes a lot of patience and endurance, but it isn't intellectually stressful. In other words, anyone can do it. But what amazes me is how quickly my children develop spiritually. Again, it is not due to anything their parents have done, but simply, by the work of God's Spirit through their hearing of His Word. My eldest was getting ready to have her first communion, and the pastor asked her what the Sacrament is and why should we desire to have it. She said, "God's body and blood is good food!" What a remarkable confession arising from the mouth of a seven year old. What an honor it is for me to be a father and to see the Holy Spirit at work in her life through my humble instruction. Again, I contribute nothing to that spiritual maturity, and find myself rejoicing in having the undeserved opportunity to observe the power and efficacy of God's word at work in the lives of new Christians. Watching my children being shaped and sculpted by the divine hands of God is, I guess, my favorite hobby. What a privilege it is to be a father. And if I feel privileged, God must feel it more, when He considers us, His children, even though it may be hard to believe.

Loving God, You watch over each and every one of Your children. Hear my prayer for my family. Preserve them in both body and soul, and help me to trust them into Your care. In Christ, my brother and Savior, Amen.

DECEMBER 19

"PADRE, I CALLED YOUR office, and you weren't there!" Big surprise. Anyone who understands the chaplain trade realizes that our ministry does not happen in our office, but rather in the corners of others' work spaces. I need to be found in the corners, for that is where God is also. He is not found on center stage. The Pharisees were so sceptical of Jesus' claims to deity. He is born in the simple village of Bethlehem, to the simple parents of Mary and Joseph (John 6:42). "We know his relations . . . we knew him as a child. He is nobody special," they laugh. Jesus' ministry of presence was deliberately off to the sides. That is where He found those who were eager to hear Him. I had a box of tracts, Bibles and rosaries inside my office. Of course, any soldier that needs to speak to a chaplain does not want to be seen coming into my office. What will the others say? So I take those same materials, put them in boxes labelled "padre," and I place them in the troops' work spaces. And they take the items, discreetly of course.

It is when I walk the lines and am on the floor that the guys will ask me that pressing religious question that has been eating away at them for years. It is in those spaces where they pull my sleeve and invite me to come around the corner to ask for advice on a crisis at home or a problem with a fellow work mate. In short, just as God has done in Christ, I do not ask them to come into my space. I go into theirs. God Himself offers the model of the most effective ministry. Why would any chaplain want to change it?

Most precious Lord, You remain present with us through Your Means of Grace. Allow me to be a means of Your grace and a bearer of Your caring presence to all those whom You place in my path, through Christ our omnipresent Savior, Amen.

DECEMBER 20

I FORGOT MY BERET for a parade. I missed calling in to my CoC after a rocket attack, again. I entirely forgot to attend a dedication ceremony in which I was to provide the memorial prayer and message. These were all my errors. I had no one to blame but myself. I simply asked forgiveness from my superiors. I could have said that there was a lot on my mind, at home and at work, and it would have worked. Certainly chaplaincy in a war zone is physically, emotionally, and spiritually exhausting. "Compassion fatigue" is a condition far too common amongst caregivers here. But today I felt fine. I had no excuses. I was humbled.

Really I don't know what I am doing half of the time as a chaplain. It is always an awkward role. I forget names, and faces. I confuse dates, and am lousy at administration. I am not as extroverted as a lot of other chaplains, so I find myself preferring to eat alone. And yet, I am told that I am an excellent chaplain. You see, just like the moment a preacher feels comfortable in the pulpit is the moment he shouldn't be there, the moment I feel comfortable in my role as a chaplain is the moment I have ceased to be an effective one. It is not simply a question of misplaced pride, but an appreciation of our vocation as originating in the Kingdom of Heaven. We ought to feel uncomfortable, insufficient and unworthy. After all, we handle the holy things of God.

In any case, I believe that we learn more from the mistakes of others than from their successes. Well, it is nice to know that I am of help to someone.

God of power, You are made known in weakness, exemplified in the humble birth and death of our mighty Savior Jesus Christ. I thank You that, although we are broken vessels, You continue to use us as instruments of Your life-changing grace and healing Spirit. Amen.

DECEMBER 21

IT WAS FREEZING TODAY. Yes, winter comes here too. The generator is broken, and so we are forced to camp all the time. We all take shifts warming our hands at the fire pit, fuelled mainly by garbage since wood is a rare commodity here. The morale of the troops is low, since our shower is a hose, and we eat ration packs three times a day. Ration packs are prepared meals in a metal bag. They have an expiry date of around forty years. They either clog up the system or clean out the pipes, depending on one's individual constitution. I can't handle more than two per day, so I usually lose a lot of weight when out on the front line with serious consequences to my immune system. And I am not the only one. Most of us are sick with flu-like symptoms. Christmas is coming, and patriotic supporters have sent letters to "any soldier" in efforts to encourage us. A lot of the letters are written by children who like to describe in detail their holiday plans. Although well intended, such letters make some of our troops miss home even more.

As a chaplain, I am used to simply being that open ear for hearing the complaints of others. To some I represent God and am the punching bag for all their quirks regarding how life has mistreated them. To a few I represent all the officers and those in their CoC who do not offer them sufficient support. To others I am simply that neutral zone; the confessional. They know that I am that confidential sounding board, who won't judge them for having a bad day. At the same time, I am also human. "He lives to hear my soul's complaints" goes one verse of the hymn *I Know that My Redeemer Lives*. Yet He can do something with that complaint. Myself, I am pretty much powerless. And on top of it, when I get impatient or snap at a Corporal, (as happened just last week when my computer caught a virus and I was put under investigation for three days) even when I apologize afterwards, the soldiers remember. I bet that Joseph and Mary weren't in the best of moods prior to that first Christmas, despite the message that they were instrumental in the birth of the Savior. Spending Christmas in Afghanistan sucks.

> *Hear my prayer, O Lord; let my cry come to You. Do not hide Your face from me in the day of my distress! Incline Your ear to me; answer me speedily in the day when I call. Amen.*

DECEMBER 22

GOD MISSES US. HE waits in anticipation for a reunion with us in His Heavenly home. Why do *we* get homesick? Our families are an extension of ourselves. They represent a piece of us. It is not natural to be away from them. Our unity is divided. I have four kids that I love, but I think I miss my wife most of all. We are one flesh, and that flesh is unnaturally separated in distance. In some ways, we are one soul. I don't mean in terms of a soul mate; someone that shares everything with you. I find that a bit creepy honestly, to be in agreement in all matters. My wife and I are very different, but are still great friends, and lovers, and have a happy relationship. But by the institution of marriage and its physical consummation, we have become one flesh, blood and spirit.

How much more is this the case with Christ and His church? Could we say that He gets homesick without negating His divine attributes? In any case, what a challenge it must be for God to hold back Christ's second coming. He must be tempted every day to stop the war, and the suffering, and be reunited with His bride forever. These were real temptations laid before Jesus by the evil one during His fasting in the wilderness. But what is stopping Him from doing it now, after all? Well, according to the parable of the wheat and weeds, the harvest is not quite ready. There are still more to be brought into the kingdom. He patiently waits for them to come, and so do the rest of us. In short, His love for humankind, that more may hear and be saved, delays His promised return. Of course, *we* would love it to happen right away, to escape our responsibilities here on earth and avoid all the pains that come with them. But, unlike God, we are selfish and lack love. Though we pray that His kingdom come in the sense of the second coming, we must always preface it by "Thy will be done." Furthermore, as Luther puts it so well, the Kingdom is already coming in the Means of Grace. Through water, flesh and blood, the Spirit of our Groom comes. So I guess God is less patient than I thought. He loves us so much that He can't wait to be near us. And so He doesn't. He visits us weekly, as we gather around His table, and He comes to us daily in the love letter of His Word.

Stir up Your power, O Lord, and come. Take away the hindrance of our sins and make us ready for the celebration of Your birth, that we may receive You in joy and serve You always; for You live and reign with the Father and the Holy Spirit, ever one God, now and forever, Amen.

DECEMBER 23

AT MOST BASES OTW the troops enjoy a weekly BBQ. This allows the kitchen staff to have a break. On the KAF, the BBQ happens once a month. Since I am the padre of several units, I get many invitations. Unfortunately we are only granted a ration of two beers or half a liter of wine each month, so I need to choose carefully with whom I will drink this precious liquid. The guys out on the FOBs get no alcohol at all, and there is no stocking up. This prejudice adds a bone of contention between those inside and outside the wire, reinforcing the idea that life on KAF is a five star resort compared to that outside. My argument is that the food on the FOBs is better and fresher, since it has a different supplier, and is managed by Canadians, as opposed to the mega cafeterias called DFACS run by an international company. Out on the FOBs you may get a *filet mignon* or even an occasional lobster or crab leg meal. After all, for these soldiers, it could be their last!

Tonight I experienced a meal at a BBQ that was memorable, but for the wrong reasons. The chicken was burnt to a crisp since there was no available lighting, and when I opened the plastic wrap that was covering the coleslaw, a swarm of flies made their escape as a new swarm took their place. It was pretty disgusting. I am not being unreasonable to be overly cautious considering the gastrointestinal issues that seem to never totally extinguish themselves. This is particularly the case during the winter months. I was told that it has something to do with the "Asian Brown Cloud," a vast cloud of fine dust consisting of feces' ash that hovers above cities in the Eastern world. This gaseous umbrella is produced by the mass burning of animal and human dung to warm homes. In the desert, wood is hard to come by. In Afghanistan, wood is precious and branches and twigs are reserved for the drying of fruit in grape huts. Even if that were not the case, the wood is so dry and dense that it is extremely difficult to burn. "You are what you . . . breathe," we joke amongst ourselves. Anyways, I was the last one to eat, as I got tied up with a member whose wife had just left him for another man. She gathered all his possessions and took off with the kids, a scenario that is far too common, believe it or not . . . sigh. I noticed everyone around me was eating the same meal. So, despite my disgust, I decided to join them. My logic: if it's good enough for them, it has to be good enough for me. And if I get sick, well, worse things could happen. Worse things: like the guys think that you are above them. For a chaplain, the implications are clear. And even during our meals or "time off" we are still always working to build bridges of trust between ourselves and the troops. A closed door in ministry is a closed door in sharing the love of Christ. My job is to be with the troops and shepherd them. And as Christ taught us, and exemplified for us, the best shepherd is the one that becomes a sheep, lives with the sheep, eats with the sheep, defecates with the sheep, and, finally, dies with the sheep. If only sheep were smart enough to avoid salad garnished with Afghan flies!

Come Lord Jesus, be our guest, and let these gifts to us be blest.
Amen.

DECEMBER 24

MANY PEOPLE THINK THAT chaplains are simply hired by the state to provide religious services to the members of the military. Our role is more complex than that, and has everything to do with military operations. We are here to assure that our members are mentally and emotionally resilient, so that they can do their job to their maximum capacity. Helping them spiritually is part of that program. Although it is a harsh way to put it, I can work within those parameters. It is, however, difficult when members forget that their personal lives do not take priority over their professional duties as soldiers. For instance, every month I have members come to see me with marriage problems and they think that they have a *right* to return home to fix them. For the most part, the military concerns itself with those kinds of problems only when they affect the member's ability to work. In such cases, a repatriation may result. Administratively we call this scenario a "compassionate repatriation" even though it is driven by operational reasons.

Can you blame the military for this apparent ruthlessness? I don't. The army is a family, but we also operate as a company, with strict budgets fixed by politicians. Many soldiers today confess that they are "in it for the money," and not the pride. It is sad to say that I remind others constantly of the difference between a soldier and a mercenary. Some get awfully close to the latter. At the end of the day, it costs a lot of money to send people home. One of my jobs is to do everything I possibly can to keep members in theater, through regulating their problems at the lowest possible level. Think about that for a moment. If you send one gunner home, it takes a lot of money and time to get a replacement. In the mean time, the other gunners pick up the slack. They get over tired and the risks to their own lives increase. The military is efficient and every position is essential. From an objective point of view, I find the military amazingly kind and compassionate to their members, although I have had my fair share of confrontations. There is a tight bond that binds members of units together. However, in our rights-based narcissistic culture, certain privileges are never enough for some. They refuse to take ownership and responsibilities for their own personal problems, and blame their respective CoC for their financial or marital failures. Of course, many of our soldiers are young men who are still maturing. The padre rightly acts as their father to help them gain control when they lack the wisdom or experience to handle the situation themselves.

Myself, I find it a privilege and an honor to serve as a chaplain, especially here in Afghanistan. I mean, who else would pay you a government wage to talk about God with young men, pray with them, comfort them, and advise them? It reminds me of working at a church camp in my early twenties. Although then, we got paid one dollar a day! This is every missionary's dream. If it just wasn't for all the rocket attacks and suicide bombers . . .

Bountiful Provider of all our needs, You warn Your people not to be ensnared in the love of riches or to seek lives of ease, but invite them in union with Your Son to live as servants in this world. Remember us when we are tempted by the allure of riches and lift us back to the things that truly matter; through Christ our priceless treasure, Amen.

DECEMBER 25

BOY, GOD IS GOOD. This Christmas Day started out pretty crummy. I ripped off a mole on my back while removing my ruck sack. Lunch was a can of tuna. And I have caught a terrible cold. But worst of all, I have been isolated for quite some time and I seriously miss the sacrament of Holy Communion. At home, I am used to a weekly Eucharist. Of course I knew before I deployed that I would be deprived of that privilege for the next ten months. Historically, fasting was broken with the sacred meal of our Lord's precious body and blood. But this involuntary spiritual fast is something that I hope that I never have to undergo again. However, a few hours ago, after conducting a service in a tent, a soldier approached me, and asked me if I was of the Lutheran Church Missouri Synod, since I had mentioned something about Luther and the Christmas tree in my sermon. I said that I was part of Lutheran Church Canada, which is in fellowship with the LCMS. With a tear in his eye, he asked me if he could receive communion with me. With a lump in my throat, I happily agreed. In a cold tent, kneeling on a sleeping bag, with a Styrofoam cup as a chalice and a Kleenex as an altar cloth, we invited the Heavenly Host to descend upon us, and feast with us, nourishing our souls with a food fit for kings.

Lord of the angelic hosts, Your angels ministered to Your Son after His time of testing and brought Him refreshment. I thank You for Your angels that surrounded me as I partook of the refreshment of His Body and Blood for my forgiveness, and for the privilege of joining with them in the singing of Your praises. In the same Christ, our Lord, Amen.

DECEMBER 26

IT WAS A FUNNY story. I shouldn't laugh, but it's hard to refrain. A Taliban was shooting at us from the branches of a tree. He accidentally misfired and shot one of his own guys, a suicide bomber on a motorcycle, who then smashed into the tree in which he was hiding. Consequently, he fell out of the tree and dropped to his death. It sounds like something out of Monty Python. I shouldn't laugh at the misfortune of others. I know that. I already confessed. But at the same time, unless you find humor in the grim moments of life here, you will sink into depression. Otherwise some days are just too long and morbid. People deal with the morbidity in different ways. Even our commanders designate all kinds of cute names for dangerous weapons, vehicles and operations. One two-tiered mission was called "Tom and Jerry," all in an effort to lighten the mood a little. Post-modern linguists and sociologists have had a lot of fun analyzing this phenomenon. Is it dehumanizing? Yes, mildly. Does it work? Yes, slightly. It is easy to judge, and intellectualize from back home. But here in the battle field and war zone, it is a totally different experience. Even the Afghans make light of the trauma that surrounds them. Amputees make the best clowns. A good gag consists of stealing the crutches of a cripple and watching him hop around on one leg, or pushing him over to see him fall on the ground. It's a different view of life and suffering: making light to bear the weight of the heavy. But it is still pretty funny—the Taliban and the tree—don't you think?

God of mercy, You know the secrets of all human hearts and You forgive the repentant sinner. Hear my prayer in the midst of both physical and moral destruction. Give me patience and hope, so that under Your protection and with You as my guide, I may one day be reunited with my family and friends in peace, tranquillity and love. Grant this through Christ, Amen.

JANUARY 2

I WROTE AN ARTICLE for a church magazine entitled *Christmas in Afghanistan* and wanted to preserve it in my journal. So here it goes:

Normally, pastors have the delicate task of encouraging people to come to church without sounding too pushy. This can get tiring after many years of ministry. The one exception is Christmas. Providing Christmas services for our Canadian Troops in Afghanistan was no different. I had the opportunity to conduct several in both French and English in some fairly remote locations. Even those soldiers that do not normally attend church, or would not consider themselves to be Christians, are more eager to hear the Word of God than we often think. But there was one immense difference. Usually, on Christmas, people tend to be in pretty good moods. After all, right before or after worship they get to go home with family, open presents, eat turkey, etc. In war, as you can probably imagine, things are very different. There is no family, turkey or presents. We have no holidays or days off. On Christmas Eve, people didn't enter the makeshift chapel (which is usually just a tent with some benches) with great big grins on their faces, chit-chatting about holiday plans with their neighbours. Neither were they particularly eager to leave chapel, since, after all, there is nowhere else to go, except back on patrol in search of insurgents and IEDs. It is all rather depressing, in one sense; which, incidentally, was the topic of my sermon that evening. I received several compliments that night, but not from bright happy faces. Somehow, compliments to pastors from expressionless faces seem more sincere. One Canadian mentioned how it was the best service he had ever attended. This was definitely not my doing. I am not the most interesting preacher, nor the best of singers. We had no musical accompaniment, candles, decorations, or a printed liturgy. All I had was a small stand-alone crucifix, placed on a table and I wore a stole. The ambiance was less than ideal for a Christmas service. Yet the soldiers were not distracted by the lack of traditional church fixings. The positive comment was a reaction to the content of the sermon, and nothing more. The Gospel was preached, heard and believed. Sadly, it is becoming less and less present in sermons today, which, can at best be considered theocentric but certainly not Christocentric. In other words, they talk about God, but not about God enfleshed in Christ for our salvation. How can you tell? Well, next time you hear a sermon, ask yourself if it would still hold together if you pulled out the message of Christ's atonement. If the answer is "yes," then the Gospel is not its foundation. It may be present, as a kind of add-on or an after thought to a long discussion of Christian morality, but it is certainly not its basis. The point is that we shouldn't be overly surprised when others are pleasantly surprised by what they hear in one of our services. It is somewhat of a new experience for many. At least for this one soldier it was.

So what did I preach about that night? The sermon began with a criticism of the sentimental expectations regarding Christmas. All the "warm fuzzies" of the popular depiction of the manger scene romanticize this monumental historical event and people. For Mary and Joseph, it would most likely have been a lonely and frightening experience: the birth of their first born, away from home, in an unfamiliar land, etc. And even after the Savior was born, and the shepherds came, and the angels sang, they were still strangers in a foreign land, trying to provide for their basic needs in the midst of a cold winter desert. The circumstances were not ideal, and emotions were probably mixed. One thing had changed, and this made the difference: Christ was there; born in a manger to die on a cross. And, as any proper Nativity scene depicts, Jesus' arms were already stretched open in infancy, to welcome all of our sins unto Him.

You probably see the similarities with our military members: they too are away from home and family; Christmas spent in a desert not that much different from that of Israel. I think the notion that hit home for that particular soldier was when I said something like this: "You probably won't leave this place tonight with a warm feeling in your heart. You may leave here as depressed as you came in. But something is different. The promise of God goes with you. The love of God that transcends any of your emotions or feelings follows you. The light of the crucified one shines in your darkness, even when you don't notice or feel it. It is a joy deeper than any sentimental experience of Christmas happiness. And sometimes, we can only come to realize that, in a place like this. For that reason, we are even more blessed than all our friends and family back home. Here, there is nothing in competition with that Gospel message; nothing to distract us from that reality. Emmanuel is present with us here. The light of the world shines in the valley of darkness, through which each of us must one day pass. However, we all know too well that the odds of passing through that valley are slightly higher for those in a war zone. Yet, that same Jesus, who was born to Mary and Joseph, is born unto you, to go with you, and go with your cross."

I realize that it wasn't the most eloquent proclamation of the Gospel, but it worked nevertheless. And, in the end, in a place like this, the standards aren't all that high and the after-service criticisms are practically non-existent. Chaplains are wonderfully blessed to be able to minister in desperate places and to desperate people, and for that reason, we are highly appreciated by our deployed troops, and so is God's Word.

JANUARY 4

Every day when I visit our hospital I am dumbfounded by the positive and committed attitude of our wounded soldiers. The comment is always the same, "Padre, I don't want to go home. I don't want to abandon my buddies!" What faithfulness! A chance to leave the war zone and return to the wife, kids, girlfriend, mom or dad, and instead, they want to stay. My responses are always something like, "you've done a great job, but now the best way of helping is going. You would want your pal to do the same, right?" That second part, they understand well. They would want their buddy to do the same thing. Go home and get well. Soldiers' love for one another is of its own category. The bonds that bind are unique. Just look at the tattoos that men and women in uniform get after a tour and choose to live with forever. These tattoos tell stories, because more happens in one year in theater and training, than in the lifespan of an average North American. May God bless these warriors for this saintly example of faithful commitment. It is an example for us Christians in the Church, who so easily abandon our religious communities as a result of conflict stemming from personality differences: the Sunday school program isn't exciting enough anymore, the new pastor has a funny accent, etc. And we are fighting a war more serious than those in the Middle East. We fight a spiritual war with Hell. How quickly we Christians are willing to abandon our sisters and brothers in arms. Most soldiers are not religious, though they are by no means disinterested in spiritual things. But isn't it remarkable how the unbelievers can be a witness, or preacher, to us believers? It wouldn't be the first time. In the Bible, the prophet Nathan is preached to by a donkey, and in the New Testament the high priest testifies to Christ's work of redemption on Good Friday. May we have ears to hear, even when the sermon happens outside of the pulpit.

Heavenly Father, may Christ our Prophet, Priest and King sustain us steadfast in our common mission of supporting our fellow Christian brothers and sisters in both body and soul, Amen.

JANUARY 8

Sometimes when we wake up, we get to hear the birds chirping. Amongst the sounds of fighter jets, gunfire and the chaos of war, the creation continues to praise God. And why should it stop anyways? Should it be silent because its stewards have decided to kill each other? Even if man ceases to acknowledge the living God, we will not be able to stop the trees of the field from clapping their hands. The birds have already been faithfully singing their hymns for thousands of years. Perhaps it is their meditation, their prayers and mediation, that intercede for us, and prevent the wrath of God from completely falling upon us all. Yesterday when I visited the Morgue, one of the Danes from Mortuary Affairs wanted to show me the secret that he kept just around the corner of the front door. He had constructed a tiny courtyard amongst the concrete barriers, in which he had planted cacti of many sorts, and one large red rose in the middle. It was the reddest rose I had ever set my eyes upon, the color enhanced due to the grey dusty background. The man displayed a great big smile upon his sunburned face. He was proud of his garden. He should be. It is not easy to make roses grow in the middle of the desert! The Afghan desert is as close as we come to the valley of death. This individual had brought life into that abyss. Working with corpses every day, ones that are so not by "natural" means, but often ripped apart by mines and bullet holes, is emotionally exhausting. This was the way in which he was able to psychologically cope with that grim reality. This beautiful happy rose in a pit of sand beside a morgue: a mix of metaphors. Such is the life that God brings forth from death. It is always a miracle. Christ crucified and resurrected present among us by water and blood, the Lord advances a new creation. This saving Creator leaves His trace even in the sparsest of places. Only one big resurrection has been recorded. But there are also small ones present everywhere we choose to look!

Lord of Life, I praise You for all the wonders of creation, and especially the resurrection power of our Lord Jesus, through whom the universe was created, Amen.

JANUARY 15

"DEATH MAKES PEOPLE EQUAL," one engineer pondered out loud. The Bible and Shakespeare have said something similar regarding the stripping down of our prestige in the grave. Although there are many inequalities in life, there are none in death, until, of course, Judgement Day. This fact ought to help us view our enemies in a proper light. Certainly, we need to kill them, but this does not necessitate that we enjoy it. There is a dignified way of terminating a life. It is a necessary evil, but an evil nevertheless. King David was not permitted to construct the Old Testament temple because his hands were bloody with the stains of war, even though the war was ordained by God. God understands the ethical dilemma. We annihilate our brothers and sisters who are fellow humans, and this is tragic, even when it is required. On the one hand it is contrary to God's will (killing your neighbour). On the other hand it is essential in establishing God's will (assuring a more stable and peaceful society for the greater good). As a Lutheran, we talk about this kind of ethical dilemma as a corollary of being *simul iustus et peccator*. Our best attempts at the good are still tainted with sin, and are, in effect, evil. Thus, we are fully sinners who do sinful things, and fully saints who, because of Christ, do saintly things. This dual-reality is echoed on a societal level as well through those who are the instruments of legalized force. Soldiers have a job to do, and it is a holy job. While at the same time, it is not a holy war. Yet even if it was, it insists upon repentance, not just from them, but from us all.

> *Lord God, remember Christ Your Son who is peace itself and who has washed away our hatred with His blood. Because You love all men and women, look with mercy on all who are involved in conflicts. Banish the violence and evil within all of us so that we may reflect our status as Your heavenly sons and daughters; through Jesus, Amen.*

JANUARY 17

TODAY, I WAS CALLED to minister to a team of grieving friends of a twenty-year-old soldier who had just died minutes before at the hospital, having stepped on an IED. The soldier was just saying that he was "going outside the wire to earn his purple heart, and pass through Germany to get back to his f@*&?** home." You need to get KIA in order to get your purple heart, and Germany is where our NATO hospital is located. It was not all that ironic that he died only hours after saying that. Soldiers almost all make the same sadistic joke when they go OTW into particularly dangerous districts. It is a coping mechanism in light of their fears. Humor, like I wrote days ago, helps us deal with tragedy, or mask our fears, at least in the short term. Those popular expressions that everyone loves to repeat,

"When it's your time to go, you go" or "When your time is up . . . ," presume that someone or something has predetermined your death date, and that there is nothing you can do to stop it. The responsibility for living is displaced onto someone or something else. This mildly brings some relief since there is not much you can do to stop yourself from getting hit by a rocket or stepping on an IED. As a Lutheran, I disagree with the notion, but I sympathize with those who say it. I, too, empathize with their fears. For me, the fear of dying is more related to my family. How would they cope in my absence? There are worse things than death, namely, the broken lives of those you leave behind. Still, even then, God can reconnect those pieces, and restore that vessel, not to its original beauty of course, but something pretty and solid, and more durable than before.

Merciful Father, our Lord Jesus Christ healed many afflicted with various diseases and pains. Show Your gracious presence to all who suffer, and help us chaplains to be agents of Your mercy through our caring presence. May all who mourn the death of a loved one find comfort and hope in the communion of saints, the forgiveness of sins, the resurrection of the body and life everlasting, Amen.

JANUARY 18

WHAT AN ODD STORY. An old Afghan man who lives in one of the most dangerous parts of our AO, has decided to dig up IEDs that he has discovered, and hand them over to the Canadians. He has already uncovered at least one hundred. He wants nothing in return! Is this guy crazy? Does he have a death wish? Or is he a local who supports our mission, and will risk his life for it? The Canadians gave him some infra-red flashers since he mainly works at night, so that we wouldn't mistake him for a target. The sad part is that this faithful soul will definitely get killed in action. He will either be shot or assassinated by the enemy, or blow himself up by the very bomb that he attempts to disassemble.

In many countries people find ideals for which they are willing to die. In a materialistic culture like Canada, where many of our ideals relate directly to our own self interest and egoism, men like this Afghan are a rare commodity. They imitate Christ, who disassembles the mines of temporal and eternal death, and sacrifices His own life in the process. Is it not strange and humbling, that the love of Christ shines through a Muslim?

Father of nations, I thank You for the courage of others, and the example that they set for me; in Jesus Christ, our hope in this life and the next, Amen.

JANUARY 19

WARDAK IS A CANADIAN Afghan who works for the military. I was responsible for his recruitment. He was an Afghan soldier who used to act as a de-miner for the UN. He ended up as a refugee in Montreal after Al Qaeda members attempted to force him to pray at the designated time. Although a faithful Muslim, he attempted to assert his right to invoke Allah and pray in his own time. Shortly thereafter, he was placed on Al Qaeda's hit list, and fled to Canada for safety. I met Wardak in one of our English as a Second Language classes offered out of the basement of a church in which I was serving as a minister. We became friends. We went swimming weekly, and he was frequently invited to suppers at our home, especially at Christmas and Thanksgiving. He had no other family nearby. Wardak was passionate about serving his country. Many cultures maintain ideals that are more important than the self. Wardak belongs to one. So does God. We often, sadly, don't. I suggested to Wardak that he apply to the Canadian Forces as a cultural adviser, even before I myself had become a chaplain. He gave it some serious thought. After I joined the military, we lost touch. Well, just a few days ago, I was talking with an interpreter and I mentioned my friend Wardak. The Afghan's eyes lit up. He knew the man, and told me that he had just finished a tour in Afghanistan as a cultural adviser. I grinned. I was not overly surprised. It made me proud. He made me proud.

Wardak is not the first Afghan that I know who has returned to Afghanistan during our mission in an attempt to support the effort to improve the conditions of life in this country. I recently met another Afghan cultural adviser who works with the Special Forces. She is related to the former royal family and her father held a high position with the government in Kabul. Due to his high moral integrity, her father fell into trouble with the leadership. In an effort to save their lives, her family fled as refugees to the United States while she was a small child. They lived in poverty for many years. At least they were safe. Despite the risks, she promised herself to return one day to Afghanistan in order to help bring positive change to her people. Her experiences and education would one day be applied through her trade, in our mission. I am proud of her too. I am proud of every Afghan who has treated his or her time abroad as a stepping stone back to their homeland. Often we ignorantly accuse refugees of taking advantage of the generosity of the system. The truth is that many refugees are often forced to remain in exile. However, there are more than a few that use their time in another nation not for personal success or advancement, but as the place from which they can work for the common good of their own nation. We are not the only ones that need to leave our country in order to serve our nation.

God Ever Just, You who hear the cry of the poor, You scatter the proud in the thoughts of their hearts and let the oppressed go free. Give us, we pray, a new heart and change our indifference to compassion. Turn our hearts towards the needs of the poor and downcast that our mouths may proclaim the Gospel and our lives mirror Your justice. In Christ, Amen.

JANUARY 21

WE CALL THEM THE "toilet crew." These are the guys who come by every day and clean our sinks and toilets. They are usually Indian or Nepalese. Getting a job like this is a golden opportunity for many of them, which is why they all jump at the chance to work on one of our bases. But the amazing thing that I find with people from South-East Asia is the priority they place on hospitality. If you go to one of their homes for supper, they will treat you as royalty, simply because you are their guest. Even amongst the Afghans, the moment that we sip *chai* together, a kind of sacred contract of friendship and trust is established. If you are invited to their home for a meal, you remain under their protection until you leave, like the angels in Sodom in the household of Lot, a man who was willing to sacrifice his daughters instead of compromising the honor and security of his guests (Genesis 19:1-8). Living in the Middle East brings a whole new dimension of meaning to the role of hospitality in the Bible, particularly that which is shown to us by Christ Jesus who invites us, His guests, to a feast in which He Himself is the cook, server and the meal.

People in the East are also a generous people. I gave one of the toilet crew a tiny pin of the Canadian flag, worth probably a quarter, and, in return, he offered me a case of pop. I gladly accepted and he gladly gave even though we both knew full well that his gift was more valuable than mine. We were both aware as well that he is paid a fraction of my salary. There is a spiritual lesson to be learned here. Namely, that the little bit that we give to God is multiplied in His grace. He offers us much more than we deserve. When we give Him an offering with no strings attached, He lavishes us with more than we could ever imagine in exchange. A U.S. study established an indirect relationship between the variables of generosity and wealth. In other words, it determined that the richer one is, the less generous one is. Perhaps this has something to do with the willingness that some people-groups express in sharing their wealth. In Christ, the King of all kingdoms adopts the poverty of all people, in order to shower upon us all of His divine wealth. The crucified King, condemned as a criminal, having the appearance of a beggar, bleeds all of His blessings upon the heads of His undeserving followers. The women at the foot of the cross, His mother Mary and His beloved disciple John, offer their prayers and praise, and, in return, He soaks them with His redeeming and atoning blood. Wow! What a sacrifice and what an exchange! Thus, "it is better to give than to receive" (Acts 20:35). Still, when we receive, the giver is equally blessed.

God Almighty, each of our vocations is holy in Your sight. May we practice our trades, carry out our responsibilities, and perform our duties in an honourable and humble manner. Forgive us for the times that we see the work of others as beneath us and carrying little value. For the sake of Christ, the King of kings, who assumed the status of a servant, washing our feet with water and our souls with blood, Amen.

JANUARY 23

THERE IS AN ONGOING debate as to whether or not a chaplain should participate in foot patrols with the infantry. Sometimes they are unavoidable. At other times, the chaplain is given a choice. Certainly, they are dangerous due to hidden mines and ground attacks, especially in the case of Canadian chaplains who are not permitted to carry weapons, nor have an assistant to act as their body guards, as is the case with the American Armed Forces. On top of that, asking the soldier at the front and behind the chaplain to keep an eye on him or her, means one less eye of surveillance on the enemy. On the other hand, chaplains add a "calming" operational presence when they accompany the young soldiers. For better or for worse, we are often viewed as a lucky charm. For instance, I remember a soldier telling me in tears, after their vehicle had hit a mine, killing two of his friends, that if I would have been there, none of this would ever have happened. I was, after all, in that same convoy and vehicle only two days prior to the explosion. For some reason, the safe completion of *that* patrol had been attributed, at least in part, to my presence with him.

Going on patrol with the troops is also an expression of our ministry of presence. It means a lot to the troops to see a chaplain with them in some of the darkest and scariest locations. I know Christ would have done it. But, then again, Christ is God, and we are not. We must be careful not to put Him to the test by careless decisions taken. The Chain of Command may make a cost benefit analysis to determine the importance of chaplain presence in the field, but they make mistakes too. In any case, today I was asked to go on patrol, and it was frightening. Yet after it was all over, all the religious questions that these 15 guys had been saving up for years started rolling out of their hearts and mouths, after they recovered from their adrenalin rushes with Cokes and smokes. I was one of the gang, and not only that, I had, somehow, become their . . . pastor! Even though it would only be for a few days, I was their pastor! The newly established relationships even resulted in a Baptism of a new Christian who no longer wanted to hold off on receiving the sacrament. With a bottle of water dumped over his head in the middle of this Afghan desert witnessed by a platoon of his soldier buddies armed for action, the whole scene was surreal. Even the agnostics among them joined the celebration.

None of these men will remember my name in years to come, but they will remember that a chaplain went with them. For better or for worse, these stories, touched by the sacred, spread. And in this case our reputation as chaplains has gained a notch in the minds of the infantry. A compliment paid to one chaplain, is a compliment paid to us all. We ride on the reputation of one another. As is the way of Christ and His church, we all benefit from the ministry of those who have gone before us. When chaplains do well, they carry the image of Christ, imprinting the same on the hearts, minds and lives of those they serve. Down the road, through each and every chaplain's intervention, we add another solid stone to those same foundations.

I remember an American chaplain sharing with me a time when he accompanied his troops in a LAV in Iraq, and the vehicle hit a mine. No one was injured, but they were all shaken up. The chaplain didn't *need* to be there. He had chosen to be there. When the guys asked him why he had made that choice, he humbly responded, "Because I love you." This is why we are chaplains.

> *Oh sing to the Lord a new song, for He has done marvellous things! His right hand and His holy arm have worked salvation for Him. The Lord has made known His salvation; He has revealed His righteousness in the sight of the nations. He has remembered His steadfast love and faithfulness to the house of Israel. All the ends of the earth have seen the salvation of God (Psalm 98:1-3).*

JANUARY 25

THERE WERE SIX YOUNG Afghan children in the ICU this morning. Kids and war will never mix well. In a way I would prefer to see a full grown man missing all of his limbs, than an infant with a bandage. I don't see too many children on the FOBs. Because they have little value in this country which has a high mortality rate, usually only the heads of the households come seeking medical treatment. After all, if the father dies, who will look after the family? A child, on the other hand, is considered dispensable. Once there was a bus accident with mass causalities. After the medics had done all that they could do to save the lives of those dumped at the front gate of their FOB, they posed the sensible question: "We see only grown men. Were there not women and children on the bus?" The interpreter replied, "Yes there were, but the locals left them on the roadside to die. They couldn't bring everybody here."

These are practical people, and, although difficult, we must reserve our harsher judgements for others. Our value systems aren't divinely inspired either. Unlike Afghanistan, in our society, little children are of the highest priority. It's something about children that moves us to pity them, their innocence, their neutrality. The kingdom of heaven consists of children. They don't deserve to suffer like the rest of us. Theologically we may assert that they too possess original sin. However, they have not compounded as many actual sins as adults. And then, in the case of Afghan children, we have the sad reality that they were, just by chance, born in the "wrong" place at the "wrong" time.

Or is it wrong? It's about grace, after all. None of us deserve good. We praise God for His grace that we were born in Canada. Logically, this implies that we question why they weren't. This is a dangerous path of reasoning. It fails to take into account both the omniscience and loving will of God. Human wisdom constantly conceals its immaturity in its neglect to grasp the true meaning of blessedness. In my experience, the eyes of the poor are more easily fixed on heaven. And this earthly pilgrimage represents only one step towards that paradise. It represents one single day in the life of eternity.

Lord God, Your own Son was delivered into the hands of the wicked, yet He prayed for His persecutors and overcame hatred with the blood of the Cross. Relieve the sufferings of the innocent victims of war; give them peace of mind, healing of body, and a renewed faith in your protection and care. Grant this through Christ our Lord, Amen.

JANUARY 26

IT WAS UNFORTUNATE. A message was sent to me. One company was looking for a few more volunteers to help facilitate an event at a local school. The local children attend the school every Saturday. Their participation depends on the time of year. During battle season they tend to stay at home since the insurgents target schools and students are viewed as sympathizers with the enemy. Each week a different unit on KAF provides a craft and a sport during the Saturday program. The email calling for more volunteers came to me. I in turn transferred it to two friends asking if they themselves were interested. Outside of my knowledge, the email was forwarded around, despite the fact that it was a personal email. Even though it clearly stated that we were searching for only 4 more volunteers, there was an overwhelmingly huge response. Everyone is always looking for something different to break up the week or month, and so the high level of interest was not surprising. I only found out about the mix-up a couple of days before the event. The guys were excited. Naturally, they were terribly disappointed when told that the majority of them couldn't go. Even though it wasn't my fault, I decided to take the blame. I wanted to save those who were negligent the embarrassment caused by a too-wide dissemination of an email.

For some reason, people are always quicker to forgive the padre than other officers. At least that is my experience. But, even knowing that, it still stinks having to break bad news. Certainly bearing that message is minor compared to delivering something serious like a death notification. But here in the theater of war, working in close proximity with others in this tight environment, the little things seem to get amplified.

Taking the blame for something you didn't do . . . hmmm. But isn't that the way of the Gospel? Christ takes the blame for our sins before the heavenly Father, and thereby redeems us of all our iniquities. What I experienced was such a miniscule humiliation compared with that of the Son of God. It gives me a greater appreciation for God's grace in light of all of my errors.

My soul magnifies the Lord, and my spirit rejoices in God my Savior, for He has looked on the humble estate of His servant; for He who is mighty has done great things for me, and Holy is His name. Amen.

FEBRUARY 2

IT IS AN INTERESTING phenomenon how, during the Commander's daily briefings, each section of his unit is represented by a seat around the table, and this includes the chaplain. In the olden days, when people belonged to churches, the Commanding Officer would expect the chaplain to offer a prayer. Some Commanders still welcome this religious element in their meetings, but for most, the chaplain has a small or insignificant role to play. Chaplains may announce religious services, put up some cute slides or thought-provoking quotes every now and again, but outside of that, they are not participants. The mission will continue with or without a chaplain. However, what I do admire is the fact that the chaplain chair is always represented. Even in cases when a unit lacks a chaplain, that seat is not to be occupied by others. It is a significant symbol of the importance of a chaplain. People notice when that spot is filled or vacant, especially during emergencies. The name of the chaplain is not recorded in that place, but only his office. It matters little *who* that chaplain is but rather *that* that chaplain is.

What a wonderful expression of pastoral vocation! As pastors we represent Christ. We are present in His stead, Christ in us, doing His work, speaking His Word, healing His people, forgiving their sins, all on His behalf. As pastors, we all do the same thing. Of course some chaplains are more popular or likeable than others. In a parish, this is even truer. But in the military, at least for those of us who are not in the Reserves, we don't normally have the opportunity or time to develop long-term relationships with people. Our identical uniforms and flaps express our common vocation and downplay our individual attributes. A cult of personality can be a dangerous thing for a pastor or chaplain, because it deflects the focus off of our Lord and His ministry and redirects it upon ourselves. It is better that the divine office of pastor is praised as opposed to any particular individual, for then God rightly receives the glory. And when people despise our godly counsel, God takes the blame, which is less personal and hurts less.

Military personnel understand this notion better than the average Christian. Innumerable people do not attend church because they have met a pastor that they didn't like. Yet I know lots of soldiers who may not have liked a particular padre, but have the utmost respect for the role of the padre. Perhaps the soil for spiritual conversion is better tilled in a military milieu than in a civilian one. The logic of the army mirrors that of the kingdom of God. Who would have thought?

Almighty God, Healer of the nations, bless all of our efforts to preach the Gospel of the forgiveness of sins through Christ to all our men and women in uniform, Amen.

FEBRUARY 4

ANOTHER CHAPLAIN AND I passed by some soldiers on the way to the DFAC for lunch. I was a bit confused because they happily greeted the other chaplain as padre, and barely acknowledged me as Captain. Officers trigger mixed feelings among our troops. I realized afterwards that the cross on my colleague's flap was more clearly defined than my own. Mine stood out less. It has happened a few times when I wear this particular flap. Soldiers have not been able to identify me as a chaplain. I appear to them as any other officer. They tend to be more polite with me when they recognize that I am a chaplain. People admire chaplains, even when they don't believe in God.

Nevertheless, sometimes I like the anonymity. It may be sad to say, but I enjoy not being recognized as a chaplain sometimes. Perhaps I feel this way too often. When I'm in a bad mood, I don't want to be known as padre, or even a Christian for that matter. I am supposed to be a light in the darkness and a positive witness of Jesus. What kind of an ambassador am I when I am miserable, tired, grumpy and a jerk? Well, I guess the honest response is . . . human. Am I not a light of the grace and forgiveness of Christ when I reflect all those less than holy attitudes? I am not a witness of saintliness in those times. I embody sinfulness; yet a forgiven sinfulness.

The robe of Christ's righteousness that covers us is not usually evident to our senses. When one is lying on his death bed dying of cancer, I have yet to experience even the most faithful Christian die "in peace," so to speak. Very few people expire that way. We usually remember the death of loved ones in the way that *we wished* that they had died, whether or not those memories correspond with reality. Eulogies are illumined by all these artificial highlights. Everyone is painted as an angel, and they go "so peacefully." In truth, normally the dying are pumped up on morphine, and they literally look like hell. But that does not change the fact, the promise, that they are all God's children, purchased and won by the precious blood and atoning death of our Good Shepherd. As a Lutheran I should understand this better than I do, that is, that the hidden righteousness of Christ is founded in a theology of the cross, as opposed to a visible one rooted in a theology of glory. Our experience in life is cross heavy, and often merits no smiles or chuckles. Real peace is not visible to the eyes or accessible by our senses. Spiritual peace is a state established by a promise of God. Peace is more than the absence of worry, just as joy is deeper than a feeling of happiness. My bad moods do not make God love me less, and my good moods do not cause Him to love me more. As a good and faithful Father, He loves me unconditionally.

"Should sin increase so that grace can increase?" Should I try to reflect a good attitude in life as a kind of witness of the Holy Spirit within me? Absolutely; especially in a negative-heavy atmosphere like Afghanistan. I should be deliberate in reflecting a positive attitude. But, try as I may, I will fail time and time again. All the artificial smiles lie heavy on the cheeks; they can become crosses themselves. When I stumble, the fact that I am still a chaplain and a Christian, not only recalls to the mind of the believer the incarnational character of the Christian Faith, but may even spark a kind of curiosity in the heart of the unbeliever: "*this* miserable chaplain is Christian?" God is good. The grace of God usually shines brighter than any light that I am capable of exhibiting in my best Christian witness. After all, the church is "full of hypocrites" . . . and there is always room for one more!

Emmanuel, God with us, I thank You for Your divine presence which surrounds me during the loneliest moments of life and for Your hands that reach towards me through the embrace of other believers; in the name of Your only Son, Jesus our Lord, Amen.

FEBRUARY 5

HERE I AM IN the heart of Taliban country. We are only a few weeks from the beginning of battle season and not far from the border of Pakistan. The insurgents find it a bit too cold to fight right now and there is less greenery available in which to hide. For better or for worse, spring is on its way. In the meantime, they survey us from a distance. They watch how we move and what we do. We find caches of suicide bomber vests and stashes of newly purchased weapons hidden in secret rooms and in walls of compounds only a few feet away. The youth are getting ready to undergo their rites of passage into manhood, which means accomplishing an act of bravery or revenge on blood feuds called "*Badal.*" In *Pashtun* culture, there is no shame in seeking revenge, cheating, stealing and killing, as long as it advances the honor of the family and clan. There are no perceived contradictions with the writings of the Islamic Scriptures. The Mullahs cannot read. Most have never attended school. The *Pashtuns* remain prey to irrational fears. And so they prepare for war. We are their enemy. We watch each other, and wait. We are all targets.

> *God of the armies, I know that war is a consequence of our sin and that we deserve nothing more from life; forgive us our sins and have mercy on us, Amen.*

FEBRUARY 8

TODAY A RUSSIAN SERVICE helicopter crashed with a team of a dozen Nepalese workers. For some strange reason, we are not as sad as we would be if it had been one of our own. What does this reflect about the human spirit? A kind of racial preference or simply a lack of sentimentalism for that which is unfamiliar to us? There is no difference in death. The workers at the Morgue show an equal respect to the bodies of insurgent causalities as they do those of the NATO Forces. Similarly, there is no rank in the grave. A general's autopsy is performed in the same manner as that of a private. That which was so precious in our lives and our careers matters so little in the grand scheme.

The treasures stored up in heaven are the ones that count more. And yet the accounting of the heavenly hosts continues to be a mystery to me. There is no distinction among humans in terms of God's unconditional love for us, and yet our Lord speaks about storing up heavenly treasures (Matthew 6:19-24). I believe that in heaven those who didn't possess many of these treasures on earth, will be provided an equal amount from the stores of Christ Himself, so that none can boast. It seems to be consistent with God's gracious character. It echoes the parable of the hired workers in which the employer gives the same pay for those who worked only an hour as he does to those who labored the full day. Are we angry that God is gracious? Are we angry that He hasn't given us all the answers to life's questions? If only all our curiosities could be satisfied. Oh how we wish we were omniscient . . . just like God. Wasn't it this kind of pride and jealousy that banned us from the Garden of Eden in the first place? "Thank God for Unanswered Prayers" is the title of a recent country and western song. The paradoxes of the Holy Scriptures keep us humble and saved, in spite of feeling insulted. Who knows what heaven will look like, and who may be its inhabitants. I am sure that there will be many surprises. We Christians might even come across some former terrorists up there, all by grace and grace alone.

> *Our Father in heaven; holy is Your name. Your Kingdom come; Your will be done on earth as it is in heaven. Give us this day our daily bread and forgive us our sins, as we forgive those who sin against us. Lead us not into temptation but deliver us from evil. Amen.*

FEBRUARY 11

IN ONE OF MY offices, there is a noticeable hole in the metal door, exterior wall, and interior wall across the hall. It was caused by a bullet. I don't know the story, but it is clear that if I was sitting in this spot on that day and during that moment when the shot pierced that wall, I would have been ripped in half. Last year I remember seeing the same thing in another office, but that time the hole was pierced through a thick window. The clerk working the desk thought it was fun to put a pencil in the hole to show the projectile line. Curiously, the bullet's place of origin appeared to be the window of a minaret!

On another occasion, a rocket smashed through the front door of a second story Canadian building, sliding down the middle corridor. It was a dud. Once again, no one was injured. Just recently, we heard the blasts of a couple of rockets, and after hearing the fire engines, we knew that it was close. It had sliced through a Canadian tent that can hold a couple of dozen people, burning everything inside, and leaving shrapnel tears in the tents around. The amazing thing was that, although there were Canadians in those very tents until three weeks ago, that tent was empty, whereas all those surrounding, were not. The concrete barriers kept the shrapnel somewhat contained. "Boy were we lucky!" Luck? Really? Coincidence? Or was it divine intervention? Of course, it doesn't explain our casualties, and we cannot know the mind of God, who, by the way, did not spare His only innocent Son in order to bring salvation to the entire world! I am convinced that if God did not put parameters around the free movement of evil, life would be a lot worse: more bullet holes in the heads of our soldiers, explosions in our buildings, and burning tents filled with people. This mission in Afghanistan gives us as much reason to praise God's mighty works as it does to repent over the extreme evils of humankind.

Lord, we thank You for Christ who surrendered His will to Yours in the Garden of Gethsemane. We praise You for the gift of freedom, and ask Your forgiveness for all the times that we abuse it. May Your will continue to be done on earth as it is in heaven, despite our efforts to the contrary; through Jesus our Rescuer, Amen.

FEBRUARY 14

"Ground hog day" they call it. Around here, every day is ground hog day. You remember the movie where the main character relives the same day over and over again. Everyday is the same here. Most personnel work 12 hour shifts with no day off in the week. Sure, if they ask permission, their supervisors will let them attend chapel, though Canadians aren't renowned for their faithful church attendance. Today is my birthday, but what difference does it make? After weeks and months in theater, the days just blend into one another. The sun goes up and comes back down, repeated again and again. Time sets a different rhythm here in Afghanistan. It is a dangerous thing to count the days left in theater. Time flows even slower when you pay attention to it.

Good Shepherd, grant me, Your impatient lamb, the ability to praise You in all circumstances and thereby follow in the footsteps of Your dear Son, the very Lamb of God who takes away the sins of the world, Amen.

FEBRUARY 18

I asked the Sergeant Major to give out dozens of "Tim cards" that I had, allowing soldiers to purchase coffee at the Canadian iconic coffee and donuts chain *Tim Hortons*, which has a satellite store here on KAF. I would have loved to give them out myself, but I have a fine enough reputation, whereas the RSM had been less popular these days for various reasons. Let's just say that he could use any help to rebuild healthy relationships with his subordinates.

A chaplain's job is to make important things happen in the shadows and not necessarily on center stage. A lot of magic occurs behind closed doors or in front of a computer screen. These are the places where chaplains advise their CoCs on delicate matters or advocate for a soldier through a series of memos of recommendations. In the same unit, there were severe problems with trust and security in the work environment. The heat of the communal stress was even felt by visitors. Although each member of the unit did a relatively good job, most did not sense support from their authorities or colleagues. They were overworked and under praised. Leadership was lacking. Some people took up smoking just to justify breaks during the work day. One section designed badges for themselves that read EWDIC, an acronym for "Everything we do is crap." Insubordination? Certainly. An effective mechanism for dealing with their stress? They thought so anyways.

The mental health workers asked me to provide weekly five minute presentations to all those in supervisory roles. The lectures covered topics such as responsible leadership, healthy communication, perceived support, etc. Slowly the workers began feeling little changes in the attitudes of those with whom they worked. Over time, noticeable changes occurred. In the corridors, I heard positive comments and healthy exchanges between supervisors and their subordinates. More jests of forgiveness and even thank yous and smiles were evident. The majority had no idea how those changes had come about. It all happened behind closed doors, orchestrated by a chaplain. No dramatic group therapy or major intervention was necessary. Pastoral counsel was all that it took to change lives. Less is sometimes more. Sure, it will never get included in my annual Chaplain Evaluation Report, the most significant document in the promotion process, or, as some have called it, the "brag sheet." But our repertoire before our heavenly Father is of far more value: to simply do the job that He has called us to do, without seeking any rewards in the process. That is the work of a true chaplain.

Lord Jesus Christ, Son of God, have mercy on me, a sinner. Amen.

FEBRUARY 25

YESTERDAY OUR BATTLE GROUP discovered a cache of around 80 weapons hidden in a home in the field near one of the Platoon Houses (i.e. tiny camps) that I was visiting. The informer was a man who had just lost his two young nephews, ages eight and nine, by an IED planted by the Taliban. The Taliban are their own worst enemies. The man, who was working with the Taliban, turned in the cache to our forces. What made him do it? Anger? Guilt? In any case, it was probably not a pure love for our mission. And yet, despite a "wrong intention" a good resulted. Think about that for one moment. God brings good from bad. It is curiously amazing and it demonstrates the bigness of God's heart. His love drives Him to delve into the world of evil in order to transform it into good. Although it is beneath a holy sovereign to associate Himself with that which is not pure. This is, after all, the message of the Christian religion. God joins Himself with the world of sinners and darkness, subjecting Himself to the worst hatred of His creation, in order to offer it salvation. Every day is "Good Friday" in the routine of our Lord as He continues to mingle amongst us and interfere with all of our bad intentions.

Lord God, teach us to number our days that we may practice true wisdom; through Christ our Redeemer, Amen.

MARCH 2

THEY ANNOUNCED IT AS the "padre limo service." I needed to get from one FOB to the next, and with haste. In response, the Air Force provided me with a private Chinook escorted by two Griffon helicopters for security. Even the VIPs rarely get *that* kind of service. God bless them!

Although many of our troops may not be believers, they appreciate their chaplain, and he or she acts a bit like a symbol of their unit pride. They are proud of their chaplain. For some, we function as that lucky charm, just in case God does exist. At least you can appeal to Him on judgement day based on the positive way you treated His chaplain. Maybe He'll cut a few years off of purgatory. For others, I like to think that the respect shown me is indicative of a spirit seeking the Lord; a kind of reverence shown to the notion of God, even by the agnostics. I can live with that. It was Fyodor Dostoevsky that said that he would rather be in the presence of an atheist than with one who is indifferent. Those who are indifferent believe in nothing, whereas the atheists have faith, even though it is not in God. They exhibit a very strong faith in a principle or idea, *albeit* of God's non-existence. When they do convert however, they make wonderfully committed Christians. The object of their faith shifts, yet their faith remains constant. Maybe this is why God says in the Revelation to St. John that He would prefer people as spiritually hot or cold, as opposed to lukewarm or indifferent.

Nevertheless, on this day, I felt like a king . . . perhaps a bit too much like Jesus on Palm Sunday, with His private escort of donkeys and warm welcome to Jerusalem, only days before His crucifixion!

> *Shout for joy to God, all the earth; sing the glory of His name; give to Him glorious praise. Say to God, "How awesome are Your deeds! So great is Your power that Your enemies come cringing to You. All the earth worships You and sings praises to You. You are awesome in Your deeds toward the children of men; through Jesus Christ, who uniquely embodies Your presence and lives and reigns with You and the Holy Spirit, ever One God, now and forever, Amen.*

MARCH 8

WHENEVER I AM IN a crowded environment where private space is hard to secure, I tell this joke: "I know how to clear the room. Just tell them that the padre is leading his Bible Study." But, thankfully, it isn't always the case. Today we had two helicopter technicians stay for Bible study while all the others cleared the canteen. We talked about God's justice, and how we often feel like we are getting short changed in life, when, in reality, we have received much more than we ever deserved. We looked at the parable of the hired hands who started working for their employer, all at different times, and they all got paid the same wage. The text said that the boss deliberately paid the last ones to start work first, and the first, last. I never noticed that part before. How the employer was totally transparent with his crew, and desired that they learn this important lesson: God is not fair, but He is generous.

In his novel *Till we have Faces* loosely based on a Greek myth, C.S. Lewis tells of a disgruntled girl that goes through life resenting the gods and keeping a record of all her complaints against them in a book. When she dies, she is brought into the great Colosseum of the gods. Her book looks a lot smaller there than it did on earth. Shaking in fear, she asks the angel, "Are the gods not fair?" The angel responds, "Oh, no, child. What would become of us if they were?"

If God were fair, we would have nothing in life, since what do poor sinful beings deserve from a holy and righteous God? What arrogance to think that we are entitled to more than we have been given (or anything for that matter). We display great ignorance regarding the meaning of grace. The hired men who started first were grateful to have a well-paying job. They were treated generously and yet were jealous to see that same generosity extended to others. The parable reveals more about our rotten attitudes than it does about God's character, except that He is so amazingly generous with us. He freely offers his unending forgiveness, love, and even physical blessings, to us often ungrateful children.

It was not an easy text for new comers, but they got the point. At first glance at the text, many remarked as to how it resembled their miserable work conditions and unfair treatment. Each one was quick to give an example. But then they saw the deeper spiritual implications. The jealousy we feel when our enemies fare well in life is unfounded. Why does God permit it? Because He loves our enemies as much as He does us! His love is never based on our good deeds or on anything good in our hearts. It is based, rather, on His grace. Theologically we call it "forensic justification": we are declared righteous by God despite anything in ourselves; a stumbling block to the self-righteousness and foolishness of those who are guided by the reasoning of the world. Remarkably, sometimes, it causes us to stumble right into the arms of Jesus, and causes us to give up our silly reasoning all-together. This is my prayer for the two that stayed, and left with grace.

Lover of humankind, forgive me when I am jealous or envious of the well being of others, and help me to mature in a faith that seeks the good of my friend and foe; in Christ who died for me as His enemy and has called me His friend, Amen.

MARCH 14

I HEARD A RUMOR recently that dozens of suicide bombers were planning on engaging in a mass attack on the KAF. On the one hand, it is rather laughable, since we would be able to see their vehicles coming from, literally, miles away. The gates are manned by Afghan soldiers, who would be at the most risk, but as far as having a significant impact on the operational life on the base of 30 000 plus . . . well, let's just say that the explosions sound more like a "thud" to most of us. On the other hand, it is terribly tragic precisely because it is absurd. Operationally, it would be pointless and meaningless. Spiritually, it may be perceived as the only secure hope for a better life in heaven. The people here are so desperate that their sole focus is on the afterlife. For a people who have been indoctrinated in fundamentalist Islam, the only promise they have of a better afterlife is through these sorts of acts of violence conducted in the name of Allah. As a chaplain, I try not to join in the laughter, although I find it difficult sometimes. Lord have mercy on me. The moment that we find the tragedy and deception of others to be entertaining, is the moment that we probably shouldn't be here. Our tasks have clouded our mission, which is to bring hope, not punishment, to all the tribes of this country.

Oh God of our salvation, Your holy Church cries out to You day and night. Let her prayers come before You and incline Your ear to her cry. Turn the hearts of both the ignorant and the unbelievers, that they too may rejoice in Your mercy; in Christ who desires not the death of the sinner, Amen.

MARCH 16

I AM CONSTANTLY SURPRISED by the religious devotion of American troops. Despite the religious trends of all the other rich Western countries of the world, most Americans are stubborn. They continue to go to church, pray and believe in the main tenets of the Christian Faith. Whenever they go out on patrol, a soldier prays beforehand. This practice is foreign to us as Canadians. However, in the past, it wasn't. In fact, our battle groups' daily operation group meeting is still called "morning prayers," because a long time ago it appears that their morning briefings were opened with an invocation and prayer to God. It was normal to ask for His help and blessing, especially in the midst of the complexities and evils of war.

Whether my officer colleagues like it or not, Morning Prayer still continues, without their permission, *albeit* in a different location. I begin most of my mornings on my knees, at my bunk bed or sleeping bag, praying for the safety of our troops and for wisdom for the leaders in our chains of command. As Luther once said in his explanation of the Lord's Prayer in the Large Catechism, the prayers of a few faithful believers go a long long way! When one Christian prays, it is as if the whole world is embraced in prayer. After all, we act as a mediator between God and others. Jesus is the Eternal Priest, and, in Him, we are a priesthood. This should motivate us to pray daily for the needs of others, even without their knowledge. In fact, prayer is one of the greatest gifts we can offer them. When we pray for them, God concerns Himself with their needs, because the requests have arisen from us who are stamped with the very image of His dear Son, Jesus the Christ. Every morning, I try to hide myself in a quiet isolated space and lift up to the Almighty, the concerns that I heard the day before. To some, prayer is judged as a waste of time, but to God it is nothing less than the goal of time. For how else can eternity be defined, other than as an endless communion and fellowship with our Triune God, *and* with all the others with whom, and for whom, we prayed?

I thank you my heavenly Father, through Jesus Christ Your dear Son, that You have kept me this night from all harm and danger. And I pray that You would keep me this day also from sin and every evil, that all my doings and life may please You. For into Your hands I commend myself, my body and soul and all things. Let Your holy angel be with me, that the evil foe may have no power over me. Amen.

MARCH 20

I LOVE THE CREW that works at the Morgue. The employees are from Holland. All of them exhibit great compassion in their trade. I noticed some tiny coffins the other day, even too small for a child. "We bury the K9 dogs in them, as opposed to bags," the guy said. The dogs sniff for mines and weapons on the front line, and save a lot of lives. On occasion they are awarded medals. Sadly, they blow up too. For those at the Morgue, all life carries value.

It must be tough working with cadavers all day long. Right outside their tiny building, the Dutch had planted a tiny Japanese garden. It is kept alive by the melted ice which preserves the corpses. Surrounded by the coldness of the concrete walls, there grow a few bushes and colorful, *albeit* dusty, flowers. Sometimes those who have lost a buddy come there and sit, reflect and pray. It is not the first time I have seen our troops plant flowers in the desert. So too, on the FOBs it is not uncommon for our men and women to keep a pet. Dogs and cats are not only useful in killing scorpions, spiders, snakes and rats, but they bring new joy and life into the temporary dwelling places. Sometimes they also carry in disease. Such was the case of a monkey brought over from Pakistan. The pets do not usually last long as a rightfully concerned Sergeant Major is going to eventually begin an extermination campaign. But what I find remarkable is the drive of the human spirit to bring light into the darkness of the most bleak situations imaginable. Normally, it isn't even a conscious or deliberate effort. As a Christian I believe that the hope of the resurrection and eternal life is somehow imprinted on all hearts, manifested in experiences like those just mentioned. Unfortunately for many, that hope is not realized; it is not even formally acknowledged. But it does give us reason to doubt the claims of early nihilists and atheists who asserted that we are solely composed of chemical compositions, that there is no God, and hence, there is no meaning in life or in death. I would argue that the meaning of life is death. Certainly, through the sanctifying waters of Holy Baptism we have a new life in union with the resurrected Lord. However, that life is hidden in the daily crucifixion and drowning of self and will only be fully realized in the Heavenly Kingdom. In the meantime, our lives are in constant preparation for our own deaths, and that which comes thereafter. If we were indeed amoral beings, the guy at the morgue wouldn't care about the disposal of an animal's corpse. Ironically, though a confessing agnostic, he is closer to God than he thinks.

Most merciful Savior, keep us from despairing in the bitter pain of death. Give us grace abounding and keep us in the Faith; through Christ the Risen who has conquered each of our deaths through His very own precious death, Amen.

MARCH 22

TODAY I RECEIVED A compliment . . . of a kind: "You are not like other padres. You don't push your religion and don't try to manage my life. You just listen and let me talk freely," said the Corporal. "I like religion too," I responded uneasily. I do have a reputation for being a good listener. Serving the French in Québec, I do not have much of a choice. Until recently, I could not understand half the conversation. However, I am not *simply* there to listen, and I do have a fixed understanding of the plan of action that the member should take to improve his or her situation. However, it takes a lot of patient listening before one earns their respect, and wins the right to speak. Maybe this was closer to what the member wanted to say.

The saying from St. Francis "Preach always, and when necessary use words" is over spoken. It can become an easy way for many Christians to avoid their responsibility of speaking about Jesus the Savior to the lost around them. At the same time, we must set the example. By listening to others, they learn how to listen to us. And it is always preferable to have the final word.

Preserve Your Word, O Savior, to us this latter day. And let Your kingdom flourish, enlarge Your Church we pray. Oh, keep our faith from failing, keep hope's bright star aglow. Let nothing from truth turn us while living here below. Amen.

APRIL 3

When every other job appears more important than my own; when I feel like it is an accident that I am here . . . Vanity! Have mercy Lord, forgive me for my high estimation and sense of self-importance. Pardon me for the concern of what others think when Yours is the sole opinion that matters, and yet the last one with which I find myself concerned. Amen.

APRIL 17

WHEN A DEAD INSURGENT arrives, a team of specialists begins to carefully search the body for booby traps. It wouldn't be the first time that an explosive device was hidden down the throat of a corpse. Isn't it amazing—the depth of evil of which the human spirit is capable? One of the arguments of the Lutherans against the Pope during the Reformation was regarding the accurate definition of the sinful nature of humankind. The Roman church believes that man's nature was wounded or bruised by the fall into sin, whereas Lutherans claim that it was totally corrupted and that nothing good remains intrinsically. After witnessing the horrors of war and incidents of hate, I think that the Lutherans have it right. Some of the best writings of C.S. Lewis are all but entirely unknown. *The Great Divorce* is one of such novels. In it, a bus load of people in hell get a chance to visit heaven because they are so miserable in their afterlife. But lo and behold, when they arrive, they are just as unhappy as before. They complain about loud music, overcrowded spaces, bright lights, etc. They hate it.

I believe that there will be fewer surprises in the afterlife than we may think. Our lives on earth reflect something regarding our love for God and fellowship with the heavenly hosts. Life is a school in which we learn to love, since, in heaven, that is what will occupy our time: loving God and others. Some are not concerned with striving for or practising love. Perhaps this is why many of the elderly seem to be either the nicest or meanest people that you will ever meet. They have either grown hotter or colder in their love over the span of their lives. Now this may be a generalization, and I realize that when one is ill and dying, it is natural to be bitter, but my observation is based on those that are in fine health. If on earth they hate God, heaven will cease to be paradise for them. They would be stuck with God and His loving ways for an eternity.

One needs to spend eternity someplace, right? God gives people what they seek. Hell represents the maximum liberty from God and everything connected to His good creation. God will no longer interfere in the lives of those who wish to be free of a relationship with Him. Accordingly, hell shows God's mercy as much as it shows His justice. In the end, we can say that people send themselves to hell, since the door to heaven is wide open to all. While outside the gates of heaven, there is only darkness and the absence of God. And sadly, that is where some people choose to belong.

Our Rock and our Fortress, You invited all people to Your wedding banquet and yet were rejected by many. May Your life-changing Gospel pierce the hardest of hearts so they can be rescued from sin and damnation. Through Jesus Christ, who rescued us from the kingdom of darkness and brought us into the kingdom of light and love, Amen.

APRIL 18

WHO WOULD SMEAR THEIR own feces on the inside of a portable toilet? Someone angry; someone having a hard time controlling his or her emotions after the death of a friend. Out in the FOBs the Afghans clean the toilets, and clean up that mess. And for a soldier who has just lost his buddy, this act is the closest he can get to showing his revenge. It isn't reasonable, but it is somewhat understandable. Shaking our heads in disgust exhibits our ignorance regarding the level of stress with which our soldiers live in the theater of war. Did you know that soldiers relearn how to breath after some combats? Their adrenalin is running so high and they are so tense, that, after a fire fight, their bodies could simply shut down. A blood rush could race straight up to their brain and kill them instantly. So, too, I can never predict the reaction of family members when I announce the loss of a child or a spouse at the front door of their home—shock, collapse—both. One chaplain was punched in the face. I have seen the wall be hit many a time. My job is to show compassion, even when it is counter intuitive. People do not choose to manifest post-traumatic stress. But, it happens, and unexpectedly.

So the next time a war veteran is found exhibiting some unusual and anti-social behavior, do not judge them. They were not always like that. Love them. Reach out to them with the arms of a Shepherd that goes out of His way to rescue the one lost sheep.

Fountain of mercy, into Your gracious and loving arms we commend all those who are sick and suffering, the hospitalized, the persecuted, the lonely, the grieving, the dying, and those who struggle with all sorts of combat stress disorders. Bring the comfort of Your Spirit to each broken body and each hurting soul; through Jesus our physician, Amen.

APRIL 21

"DOG TAGS." WHAT A brutal connotation. Despite the dehumanizing metaphor, these tags are the identification collar of the soldier. When our pets get lost, they can't speak, and so that tag around their neck is their only hope of being found by their owners. And so too, the unconscious, injured and dead are unable to speak. They can't inform others of their blood type so that a life-saving transfusion can be carried out, or tell of their Faith group so an appropriate prayer is said. When they lack the capacity to speak, that piece of metal does.

The Revelation to St. John talks about us being marked by the blood of the Lamb. We are, in a sense, tagged by God, and He does the talking when we can't. There is a great security in this. It reflects an ownership. Just as I am a possession of the Army, so too I belong to the Kingdom of God. I am tagged in my Baptism, with a heavenly citizenship secured. As a reminder of this promise, along with my dog tag I wear a pewter cross on the same chain. It says, "*Je suis avec toi,*" on the reverse, meaning "I am with you." I belong to God, purchased and won by the atoning death of Christ on the cross. I may not know what the future holds for me, but He does, and I am in His hands. His hands are, after all, more reliable than my own.

Gentle One, Your Son does not quench the smoldering wick. Remember in mercy all those who struggle with fear and doubts, and strengthen them through Your Word and promises; in Christ, Amen.

APRIL 24

RECENTLY, I WAS MISTAKEN for a medic. Medics and chaplains both wear a cross on their flaps, although the designs are slightly different. At first I corrected the individual stating that "I was *just* a chaplain." Then I corrected myself again and commented that my trade does involve healing: spiritual healing. The church is, after all, a hospital for sick sinners. The soldier rolled his eyes and walked away. Incidentally, I have heard it said that the Taliban will pay the highest price for a captured chaplain. We are right up there with the K-9 dogs (who are our greatest resource for sniffing out explosives). For some, the chaplaincy is the least important trade; for others, it is one of the most important.

Jesus is the Great Physician, and many walked away from Him and even chased Him out of their villages. After telling His Jewish disciples that His flesh is salutary and that drinking His blood offers eternal life, St. John tells us that many of them departed (John 6:66) . . . but not all of them. Jesus stuck around for the others. He came for the one lost sheep; for the one sick soul. What leads me to think that I as a Christian chaplain, who follow in His footsteps, should expect anything more . . . or less?

Jesus Christ, my ransom from death and darkness, give me the same love for others as You have for me, and enable me to consider it a blessing when rejected because of it. Amen.

MAY 8

WAR TOURISM. IT'S A term coined here that describes some of the VIPs who come from North America to Afghanistan in order to satisfy their curiosity. Perhaps the term is a little harsh and unfair. Undeniably, there is something unsettling about the phenomenon. At home something similar occurs at the scene of a car accident. The traffic slows down on the highway. This does not primarily reflect philanthropic concern. Few are actually interested in the welfare of the unfortunate injured drivers, but rather they are curious to see the damage, and maybe get a glimpse of some blood. I am guilty of this as well. As much as I try to look away out of respect, I can't resist the temptation to sneak a peek. It is sick, I know. This is somewhat less of a temptation in the theater of war. One of my jobs is to minimize unnecessary exposure to corpses. Grotesque images can leave permanent traces in our minds. In the case of a fatality, and when I am asked to offer a prayer, I take great care in controlling where I look. The eyes are, after all, the window of the soul. If the blanket is already pulled over the deceased or the body bag is already zipped up, I leave it like that, even for a blessing. This kind of sensitivity and precaution serves as an example also for all the younger soldiers.

So what is it that these "war tourists" hope to see anyway? I think they want the experience. They want to wear the gear, fly in the choppers, ride in the clips . . . just for a bit. So they can tell their families back home how cool it all was . . . even better than a video game!

*Everlasting God of Truth and Purity, all the inclinations of man's
heart are evil; forgive our childish ways and help us to store up
treasures in heavenly places; through Christ our King, Amen.*

MAY 25

SOMETIMES I FEEL PARTICULARLY sorry for our enemies, even knowing
full well that they work for Al Quaeda or are Taliban. Take for instance,
when we capture them. Seeing them ear muffed, blindfolded, loaded onto
a helicopter, and hearing about them defecating in their pants or vomit-
ing out of fear, would touch even the hardest of hearts. Most of them
have never ridden on an aircraft. Some of them are young kids who are
working with insurgents for the money. Others have lacked any opportunities to critically think or judge, and, in short, are simply brainwashed
into siding with the insurgency. It is the only life they have ever known.
And though we are sent here to improve their lives, we are still strangers
who import a foreign culture of food, smells, clothes, etc. Their identities
stretch centuries into the past, isolated from Western culture. Christ says
that we are fighting not flesh and blood but powers and principalities,
which is entirely true. The only problem in war is that we can't imprison
the devil and the demons, but can only deal with those through whom
they act. However, that does not preclude our prayers for them, and for
repentance and peace. And at the end of the day, we would probably be-
have as they do, if raised under the same circumstances. In fact, we are
not that different. In the West, we simply have a more sophisticated supply of resources to help manage and control that evil which is impartially
present in the heart of every human being.

*Jehovah, God of gods, You created all people in Your image and
have commanded us to love the least of people and even our
enemies because they bear the imprint of Your holy face. A Desert
Father once advised, "May we live our lives as if only I and God ex-
isted." May Christ, who is Your image and has stamped His image
upon us through Your Means of Grace, enable us to treat others,
even the worst of humanity, as bearers of Your presence, helping us
to live by faith and not by sight. Amen.*

JUNE 2

PEOPLE NEED THE LORD. I think that that was the title of a Keith Green song many years ago. The phrase strikes me especially as true whenever I make my hospital rounds. People that would normally not make use of a chaplain or pastor are more open when sick or coping with anxiety. On numerous occasions I have had Mormons and even Muslims ask me to pray for them, in full awareness that I pray as a Christian. "That's okay chaplain, I'll take whatever you've got!" A beautiful kind of desperation is reflected in that attitude; an acknowledgement that you cannot make it on your own—that somehow the chaplain carries Good News and the presence of God.

Even among recovering patients, I find the reception of a chaplain warm. Perhaps patients are bored and are prepared to talk with just about anybody to make the time pass faster. Even if that is the case, I'm okay with it, because, one way or another, the conversation always ends up in questions involving the Faith. Unlike Americans who are more forward with their invitations, Canadians and Europeans remain more reserved. Despite appearances, I firmly believe that underneath any stubbornness and resistance, the desire for a divine word is still there. Sometimes God is not mentioned in our bed side exchanges. However that cross on our flap speaks louder than words, and assures those proud yet fragile souls that God is not our enemy, but graciously present, despite the lack of any formal invitation.

Great are You Lord, and greatly to be praised, and Your greatness is unsearchable. I thank You for Your commitment to showing us grace, being slow to anger and abounding in steadfast love. May Your mercy continue to extend over all Your creation; in the name of Jesus, Amen.

JUNE 8

I RECENTLY BEGAN SENDING out a weekly chaplain message to all the members of my units, with information regarding religious services, explanations of religious holy days, a light-hearted joke, and some mental health resources on anger management, sleep, stress, etc. I also include some quotes from famous religious figures. Certainly, I am careful which citations I include, and I ensure that they are not in contradiction with my own beliefs, but reflect the wisdom of the Old and New Testaments. Now I fully recognize that the majority simply delete the emails along with all kinds of other intranet mass messages. But for a few, my quotes are the highlight of their week. They eagerly wait to read what the padre has posted this time. Those who comment on my messages are not confessing Christians. They are seeking and thirsting for wisdom. These quotes offer them a peek into the world of spirituality and a crack in the door of the church. Why else do the *Chicken Soup for the Soul* books and other self-help pop psychology sell so well? Along with Dr. Phil and Oprah, they are the confessionals of the modern age. Clearly, a peek does not suffice. Yet that peek may turn into a glance, and that glance may turn into a trance: that holy obsession with Christian wisdom that we may as well call "Christian conversion."

Creator God, I thank You for the arts and their ability to creatively convey the Gospel of Christ the Crucified to the confused and the lost, Amen.

JUNE 24

A DIRECTIVE JUST CAME out that asked us to return or dispose of all crates of bottled water from one particular provider, because they had become mildly poisoned by sitting out in the sun for too long. Now, in KAF we have about 30 000 people drinking about 12 bottles of water a day. There are only three companies that supply us. You can do the math. It represents a lot of wasted water. What a strange sight. Here in the desert, where water is such a precious commodity, we are asked to dump it out. What irony! It made me think of how true doctrine, the moment it is perverted by falsity, is poisoned, and ceases to be useful as spiritual drink. The instant that the precious Gospel is compromised, when works of man are added to faith as salutary, the divine system of salvation grinds to a halt, and does not simply absorb some minor damage. What care our military takes to keep us healthy and its equipment in top shape. Christians could profit to do likewise. Now *most* of that water was still safe to drink. But *some* of it was potentially deadly. Accordingly, *all* of it was dumped. If only the Church would mimic that kind of caution. Often our congregations have little interest in questions of doctrine and our true spiritual health, as they obsess themselves with the future of their buildings, the absence of young people in the pews, challenges of finances, etc. All these fears would be put to some rest, if we rightly prioritized our values, as they do in the army.

Good Teacher, may we abide in Your Word and treasure Your doctrine that leads us to life eternal; through Christ who has justified us by grace through faith, Amen.

JUNE 29

How I THIRST AND starve for another chaplain of my own religious confession. Don't get me wrong, I get along great with my fellow chaplain co-workers, but there exists an irreplaceable brotherhood between those of your own faith group. One of the hardest challenges of being a chaplain is finding a way to provide for your own spiritual care. Unlike some Christian denominations in the Canadian Forces, Lutheran chaplains are not numerous. This poses some difficulties in assuring spiritual care for oneself and one's family. Besides the Sundays when I conduct a Lutheran Eucharist at a Base Chapel, or when I visit a Lutheran church on holidays, I am rarely exposed to the Lutheran Divine Service. In Québec, where I am presently posted, protestant churches are few. I was well aware of this when I joined the Canadian Forces, but I never realized how much I would miss parish life and the fellowship of Lutheran communities. In a way, at home, my family has become my church, and I have become my own church here. It is discouraging, but God is good. He still provides. A few nights ago, after conducting a service for about 12 people, one stayed behind. He said that he was Lutheran, and asked to commune with me. What joy! God promises to give us whatever we ask for in His name and according to His will. And what gives God more joy than to offer His Flesh and Blood into the mouths and hearts of hungry believers?

Father of all, continue to shine in our lives by Your precious Word and Sacraments, which enlighten our lives and strengthen our faith, through Jesus Christ our Lord, Amen.

JULY 21

AFTER COMING BACK FROM R&R (i.e. Rest and Recreation of a two week vacation) we receive in-theater briefings that act as reminders of our SOPs, just in case we forgot some of them during our short time away. Most of the briefings are refreshers regarding combat first aid, IED detection, etc. There is one, though, that emphasizes the importance of not throwing out batteries since the enemy can search through our garbage and use old batteries to construct explosive devices. Old cell phones are commonly manipulated to act as a remote control detonator. At the FOBs, that garbage which we cannot burn we ship out to prevent any locals from having the opportunity to snoop through it. All paper documents are incinerated or shredded, even on KAF.

It is a sickening feeling to think that a thoughtless act such as throwing a used battery in the garbage could indirectly lead to the death of a fellow soldier. It is a powerful reminder, however, that we are all responsible for the suffering of one another. As the physics of fragment theory have taught us, all events are connected somehow, somewhere. We cause the suffering of others without any cognisance. So much for the claim that "I am a good person . . . I never killed anybody." How do you know? Perhaps that car you cut off ended up in a fatal accident behind you, and you never even knew it!

Consider Afghanistan: due to one tiny error on the part of the British Commonwealth, the country has been practically in a state of civil war between the North and South ever since. Failing to take into consideration the complex regional diversities within the sociopolitical cultures and languages, the English drew lines on a map, creating an "artificial" country. The borders do not reflect the geographical-political realities of the people, who refuse to, or are incapable of, respecting them.

We all share the sin of the world. We are all responsible for the burdens of one another. And so, just as through one man entered sin . . . through another man we have life (Romans 5:12).

Lord God, no one is a stranger to You and no one is ever far from
Your loving care. In Your kindness watch over refugees and victims
of war. Because their status has often been indirectly caused by
our ignorance and selfishness, forgive us; in Christ, our Redeemer,
Amen.

JULY 23

IT IS MORNING. THE Mullah calls for prayer from a speaker beside my tent. The Afghan army and police with whom we work rise to invoke the name of Allah. I can never sleep after that. I wake up to do my own prayers, and get to see many sunrises over the eastern mountains. The colors are remarkable. I refuse to take pictures because they cannot do it justice. They will only spoil the memories. I have travelled to many countries during my life as a pastor and chaplain. One thing I know for sure: all sunsets and sunrises reveal any place as beautiful. Afghanistan is no exception!

God of creation, Creator of all life and provider of all good things, the hills, trees, birds and even these desert rocks praise Your holy name. Guide us all to become better stewards of this earth and caregivers of our fellow brothers and sisters in humanity, that we may join in the joyful song of praise; in Jesus Christ our happiness, Amen.